BLISS,

Not

BURNOUT

PRAISE FOR *BLISS, NOT BURNOUT*

"High praise for *Bliss, Not Burnout*! This book is a must-read for anyone who finds themselves behind a desk (in an office or at home), in a health care setting where awkward angles and locked legs are a "thing," and out in the field where ergonomics don't matter when you're trying to give the best care possible. Take care of yourself, dear superhero! Let *Bliss, Not Burnout* show you how!"

— Wayne Pernell
President of DynamicLeader Inc.
Elite Mindstate Coach and Bestselling Author

"Dr. Roberta Garceau has crafted a beautiful masterpiece with *Bliss, Not Burnout*. She infuses her witty anecdotes with comprehensive tools for preventing burnout, a concept increasingly researched and discussed in our hasty modern-day world. Garceau gives her readers suggestions to implement that will enhance our lives and allow us to thrive, not just survive. Practical and tangible concepts of our dosha compositions and how to maintain equilibrium with them through breathing, sleeping, food choices, etc, are presented thoroughly and concisely. This book has thoughtful strategies and tactics for health care providers as well as any person hoping to achieve balance in their lives. If we can put the work in our own minds and bodies using *Bliss, Not Burnout*, our world around us will flourish, led by the changes within us. Thank you to Dr. Roberta Garceau for allowing the Connecticut Academy of PAs to have early access to this insightful book. We look forward to applying these approaches to our own lives to bring more peace to ourselves and those around us."

— Cayla Daniele, PA-C
President of the Connecticut Academy of Physician Assistants

"A compelling mind-body journey from a dentist who made some fascinating discoveries about how we can all stay healthy and reach our potential."

— Dr. John Douillard, DC, CAP
Āyurvedic Author, Founder of LifeSpa.com

"*Bliss, Not Burnout* is not your typical book about how to navigate your life and all of its overwhelm. This is a very personal call to action from a woman who wants to help you help yourself. Roberta Garceau shares her extremely vulnerable journey in service of your health and wellness because she knows what's at stake—your life. It's part wellness guide and part memoir, calling on the ancient yoga and ayurvedic practices in service of you making a change today. I highly recommend this beautiful book and that you reach out to Roberta, who invites you to do just that at the end of her book."

— Tricia Brouk
International Award-Winning Director, Author, Producer
Founder of The Big Talk Academy

"You hold in your hands a practical guide to nourishing yourself, rooted in the modern and ancient wisdom of mindfulness, science, and practical experience, full of stories from Dr. Garceau who has a compassionate understanding of the realities of being a health care provider in a demanding culture. She not only provides wisdom, she provides deep inquiry and pragmatic tools that lead back to wholeness. *Bliss, Not Burnout* is ultimately a manifesto about the permission that self-care is not selfish, but self-fulfilling."

— Erin Casperson
Director of the Kripalu School of Āyurveda

"One of the great benefits of my role in mentoring workshop leaders, who are also authors, is to see the creativity of their full expression in a book like this. *Bliss, Not Burnout* answers an unmet need in our current epidemic of stress for frontline providers. It's truly a valuable addition to the field of self-care for burnout prevention. Roberta's emphasis on self-awareness rings true to all that we know from research in modern mind-body medicine, as well as from the ancient wisdom traditions. Thoroughly researched and grounded in practical applications, it's a user-friendly reference and go-to field guide for frontline caregivers."

— Ken Nelson, PhD
Author, Kripalu Yoga Legacy Teacher
Mind-Body Educator, Workshop Teacher-Trainer

"An invaluable guide for health care providers, blending the wisdom of āyurveda and yoga with the demands of modern medicine. This book offers essential guidance to prevent burnout, strengthen the immune system, and foster self-awareness through practical tools like asana and pranayama, making it a vital companion for anyone dedicated to compassionate caregiving. It's packed full of resources designed to empower health care providers to better serve themselves and their patients."

— Larissa Hall Carlson, MA
Āyurvedic Practitioner, Āyurvedic Yoga Specialist
Former Dean of the Kripalu Schools of Yoga & Āyurveda

"Roberta Garceau has thoughtfully crafted this practical and insightful guide from hard-earned personal and professional experience and years of study. She integrates multiple traditions and approaches in a unique tapestry of concepts, reflection exercises, daily practices, encouragement, and real-life stories. For anyone wanting to bring more wellness and ease into their life (and avoid burnout!), this book provides a gold mine of ideas that promise to renew, restore, and bring real and lasting change."

— David Ronka
Author, Trainer, Coach

BLISS,

Not

BURNOUT

Hope for Health Care Providers

Dr. Roberta Garceau

Publishing support provided by
Ignite Press
55 Shaw Ave. Suite 204
Clovis, CA 93612
www.IgnitePress.us

ISBN: 979-8-9915850-0-2
ISBN: 979-8-9915850-1-9 (E-book)

For bulk purchases and for booking, contact:

Roberta Garceau
roberta@drrobertagarceau.com
www.drrobertagarceau.com

Because of the dynamic nature of the internet, web addresses or links contained in this book may have been changed since publication and may no longer be valid. The content of this book and all expressed opinions are those of the author and do not reflect the publisher or the publishing team. The author is solely responsible for all content included herein.

This book is not intended to be a substitute for professional medical advice. It should not be used to diagnose or treat any medical or psychological condition. Readers are advised to consult their own medical advisors, who are responsible for determining the reader's condition and best treatment.

Library of Congress Control Number: 2024918962

Cover design by Usman Tariq
Edited by Cathy Cruise
Interior design by Jetlaunch

FIRST EDITION

This book is dedicated to my dad, Gerald Garceau, for teaching me by example the values of gratitude, respect for all living beings, and love of family, friends, and community.

ACKNOWLEDGMENTS

I'd like to thank all those who helped *Bliss, Not Burnout* come to fruition. Big thanks to Tricia Brouk, Erin Casperson, Cayla Daniele, John Douillard, Larissa Hall Carlson, Ken Nelson, and David Ronka for giving generously of your time in reviewing the unedited manuscript, providing valuable feedback, and endorsing *Bliss, Not Burnout*. Your contributions enhanced the quality of this book immeasurably.

Special thanks to Wayne Pernell for reading with a fine-tooth comb, always delivering authentic feedback, and offering the Foreword. Your coaching has not only helped me navigate through the logistics of publishing, but also to dream bigger in life. I appreciate the ways you've supported my growth.

For the yoga videos and still photos, thank you Tobias Baharian of CT Video Production. I appreciate your creativity and willingness to explore different energies in nature while capturing the essence and intention of *Bliss*.

Thank you to the amazing team at Ignite Press: Everett O'Keefe, Zelda Fogle, Malia Sexton, and editor Cathy Cruise. Your guidance has been instrumental in converting *Bliss* from a document into a living, breathing, transformational product. Thanks also to Paula Pierce, Janine Bolon, the team at Hosting CT, and everyone who helped to get the word out so more people have access to *Bliss*.

To my teachers in dentistry, sleep medicine, yoga, and Āyurveda, thank you for expanding my understanding of wellness and what is possible. You are too many to mention, but your dedication to perpetuating your craft is priceless.

I am grateful for you, dear health care providers, for boldly and vulnerably sharing your stories and your truth. Thank you for the work that you do in caring for others. *Bliss, Not Burnout* is more meaningful and impactful because of your participation.

As for my students and patients, thank you for entrusting me to be your teacher and health care provider. You have taught me more than you can imagine, challenging me to be a better teacher and health care provider every day.

To the incredible women with whom I have had the privilege of providing holistic dentistry and sleep medicine, thank you for your willingness to grow with me. Together we practice Elemental-Wellness and positively impact countless lives.

As for my family of origin, thank you for bestowing your sense of humor and humility! You taught me the virtue of gratitude, and you continue to help me to feel loved, supported, and grounded. This journey and learning process has brought me back to my roots, to what is real and true.

To my extended family—including my family through marriage—and my dear friends, your support fills the wind beneath my wings! You are my cheerleaders. You know who you are.

To our children, Jacenda and Liam, words fail to describe how blessed I feel to be your mom. You have stretched me to be a better human. You bring me boundless joy, and I am so proud of the beautiful beings that you have become.

And Jerry, my husband of over a quarter century, thank you for making me laugh, for grounding me when I get overwhelmed, for believing in me even when my dreams seemed hard to understand, and for giving me your love, respect, and support. Beyond a doubt, you have helped me to be a better version of myself.

AUTHOR'S NOTE

The contents of this book are not meant for self-diagnosis or treatment of any medical condition and do not constitute or serve as a substitute for professional medical care. The knowledge herein is intended to supplement and complement modern medicine. I offer no panacea, nor do I recommend any one-size-fits-all diet or exercise regimen. My background as a practicing holistic dentist, a certified yoga and āyurveda instructor, and a diplomate in dental sleep medicine, combined with life experience, inform the material within these pages. I am an imperfect middle-aged woman with an imperfect body. Why would you be interested to read on? This book is an invitation for you to explore and embody even one or two small concepts that resonate with you so that you can live a life of expanded wellness. If you are a health care provider, you give abundantly to your patients, your loved ones, and your community. You care for others even at the cost of your own well-being. You deserve to be well and to enjoy your best life. This book is an invitation to access your inner wisdom, using a personalized combination of strategies in order to enjoy greater health and well-being.

TABLE OF CONTENTS

Foreword by Dr. Wayne Pernell xvii

Introduction xix

Chapter 1   Unexpected Gifts 1

Chapter 2   Work-Life Balance and Self-Awareness —
             Keys to Achieving Bliss, Not Burnout 5

Chapter 3   Physical and Mental Health 15

Chapter 4   Integrative Medicine — The ABCs of Elemental-Wellness:
             "A" is for Āyurveda 25

Chapter 5   "B" is for Breath and Breathing 45

Chapter 6   "C" is for Connections, Caregiving, and Communication 53

Chapter 7   "D" is for "Daily" (Dinacarya) and Diet 65

Chapter 8   "E" is for Exercises 81

Chapter 9   "F" is for Fun Favorites 119

Chapter 10   "G, H, I, J" are for Gratitude and Grace, Harmony,
             Intentionality, and Journaling. 135

Conclusion: Putting It All Together 147

Review Inquiry 149

Will You Share the Love? 151

Would You Like Roberta Garceau to Speak to Your Organization? 153

About the Author 155

FOREWORD

I tried yoga once. It was too much of a stretch for me.

My joke became my way to avoid joining others in a class or even trying something that moved my body in a way that I hadn't really explored consciously before. As kids, we move, we stretch, we just do what we do in the moment. I'm a fourth-degree black belt in the martial arts. My body used to do amazing things. I do believe that I can get my flexibility back. It's going to take some true attention because now, as adults, when we are in service to others, we don't tend to move as we did when we were younger. We hold our bodies in truly unnatural positions—sitting, leaning, or standing lock-kneed. This is how we show attention to others. And it's killing us.

Burnout comes from many different directions. There are all kinds of stressors in our lives. Each of us has our own unique blend that we manifest. Sure, the foundation for stress is all around us, but what if . . . what *if* . . . we chose to be in the world just a bit differently? What if we chose to shift from DIS-Stress to EU-Stress? What would happen if we chose to respond to the world in a way that everything that happened had a positive effect on us because we wanted it to?

Here *Bliss, Not Burnout* takes us through some of Dr. Roberta Garceau's personal history. Through sharing some traditional strategies and practical tools, we as readers are invited to tiptoe into trying out some different steps to take in our lives. From mindset to movement, you'll find a personal yet practical path to finishing your day, week, month, and year smiling. After reading the manuscript for this beautiful book, I had a conversation with Roberta and told her, "I can't *do* some of the things you're asking for in Chapter 8." Thereafter came the gentle reminder that this is a book of self-awareness with permission and encouragement to honor yourself, moment to moment.

Do what you can.
Practice what you're able.
Build on those.
Observe as your body leans into doing more.

We all want to serve more greatly. You can't give what you don't have, so it's important to fuel your mind *and* your body. These wonderful pages ahead will indeed guide you to *Bliss, Not Burnout*.

— Dr. Wayne Pernell
President, DynamicLeader Inc.
Elite Mindstate Coach and Bestselling Author

INTRODUCTION

As a practicing dentist for over 25 years, I've embraced modern science and medicine as we know it today. Believing in the importance of continuous learning, I pursued a residency and fellowship in general dentistry upon graduation from dental school, attained fellowship in the Academy of General Dentistry, and continue to study the latest advancements in the field in order to bring my best to my patients and my team. From the beginning, I appreciated the connection between oral and systemic health, as well as mental and emotional health. For years my mission has been to help others improve their health, function, self-esteem, and overall well-being. That's holistic and compassionate care, and it's the only way I can imagine practicing. Helping patients to be comfortable, seeing them overcome their fears, and enjoying a smile that they never thought could be possible is so rewarding—and I'm blessed to get out of bed and be able to do this every day!

As the youngest of seven siblings, I've had the distinct privilege of witnessing each of my brothers and sisters suffer from back issues over the years. Hoping to avoid the same fate, I sought techniques to strengthen my core and protect myself from work-related injuries. This brought me to investigate yoga as a means to greater physical health.

I basically dabbled in yoga for about two decades—being the owner and full-time practitioner in my dental practice, as well as a mother of two young children and juggling all of life's other demands, I was never a very regular or devoted yoga student. That is, until one morning, in the wee hours before our children woke up (before we had to scurry around the house to get everyone to daycare and school and work), when I was in the dark of our basement practicing the same prerecorded yoga class (okay, it was a DVD back in the day!) for a mere 25 to 30 minutes, that I experienced a physical response like no other. I felt like I'd just had the best massage of my life, and the beautiful thing, I realized, is that I had just given it to myself! Practicing over time, even just 25 to 30 minutes once or twice a week, I began to notice some other unexpected results: greater calm, enhanced peace, more stable physical and mental grounding, sharper focus, and clarity. Surely there was something to this "woo-woo" yoga hippie thing!

In time, I was called to become a certified yoga instructor, and I began to appreciate the potential for not just physical and mental health, but also emotional/spiritual/energetic healing. As a newly minted instructor, I donated my services to teaching adults who were in recovery, at risk of homelessness, or struggling with mental health issues. When the opportunity presented itself to become certified in Yoga4Cancer (y4c), I became part of a research project where I taught yoga to patients who were in treatment for or recovery from cancer, witnessing their struggles with neuropathy, scar tissue, and diminished immunity and energy. In my work community, I shared yoga with adults with intellectual and physical disabilities—they proved to be some of my greatest teachers! On and off the mat, my mission was the same as in dentistry: to lift others to empower themselves and to enjoy greater health, function, self-esteem, and overall well-being.

Back in the land of dentistry, I was becoming more and more aware of the role of healthy breathing in one's complete health, and how modern medicine had virtually neglected this critical component of wellness. I learned how snoring and sleep apnea (collectively known as sleep-related breathing disorders) increased the risks of heart disease, stroke, diabetes, Alzheimer's, depression, anxiety, thyroid disease, erectile dysfunction, and more. Reviewing my dental patients' medical histories, I began to see both the risks and consequences of untreated breathing disorders: uncontrolled high blood pressure, heart attacks, ADHD, insomnia, etc. My comprehensive dental examinations evolved to include greater awareness and screening for potential breathing difficulties, which often were unbeknownst to the individual. I began to see the head and neck physical traits (narrow dental arches with crowding, long or large necks, enlarged or elongated uvulas, cryptic tonsils, large or tongue-tied tongues) that predisposed a person to breathing difficulties or suggested that they might be at risk.

Realizing how much there was to learn, I furthered my education and became a diplomate of the American Board of Dental Sleep Medicine. In the process, I cultivated relationships with local sleep physicians and providers to better help our mutual patients. For many, the results were transformative: a woman in her 40s was finally able to sleep in the same bed with her husband after over 20 years! Another woman in her 50s, who was severely depressed, frequently physically ill, and in danger of losing her job, found energy and wellness again. Even a male physician colleague who didn't think he had any breathing trouble (but got tested because he developed atrial fibrillation and realized it could be caused by sleep apnea!) found that he awoke more refreshed and rested without his alarm clock and had more energy throughout the day. Life as a comprehensive and holistic dentist with a focus in dental sleep medicine was deeply rewarding. We were improving our patients' quality of life and also saving lives.

I continued to study various styles of yoga, and then somewhere on the way to my 1,000-hour teacher training, this strange phenomenon called a pandemic happened! Being a perennial student who has always been interested in growth, learning, and continuous improvement on a daily basis, I was frustrated with the lack of educational options in both the yogic and dental worlds. Whatever was available then was only being offered online. With much of the world shut down, and prior to mass vaccinations, in-person learning was not an option.

Then one midsummer day in 2020, I saw an email from the Kripalu Center for Yoga & Health offering a 75-hour online class, Uniting Yoga and Āyurveda. While I had reservations regarding what the experience could be compared with in-person instruction, I was hungry to learn and had little to lose, so I signed up. While I had been exposed to bits and pieces of āyurveda in my yoga training, this was my first significant immersion in its history, medicine, and philosophy. The class exceeded my expectations, and at the conclusion, there was an invitation to dive deeper—a 200-hour online course in the foundations of āyurveda.

Ha! There was no way in Hades I was signing up for that one, thank you very much! After all, I was still trying to get my dental practice back on its feet after being shut down from the pandemic, my children were still largely learning remotely, and my nonagenarian mother, who was still grieving the loss of her husband/my father only six months earlier, was having significant health issues. Certainly taking this class at this time made no sense. And yet, one of my Uniting Yoga and Āyurveda classmates from across the country encouraged me to sign up. "It will be life-changing," she said, "It will completely change the way you practice dentistry." Well, I was doubtful about that, and yet just two days before the class was to begin, I found myself calling and signing up!

Learning about this ancient medicine and its wisdom from thousands of years ago, which is still practiced today, was eye-opening, to say the least. I was struck by how seemingly simple and simultaneously complex this understanding of life (literally "Life Wisdom") could be, particularly since it originated prior to the invention of the microscope and before our understanding of microbes and subcellular structures. Little by little, I began to adopt simple practices and "tweaks" in my daily life. The beauty was that no one was asking for a seismic shift or really any change at all. I mean, it's human nature to avoid the effort of change. But when one considers just a tiny tweak or shift in routine, it's not so daunting, and the results can be pretty rewarding!

How does my personal journey lead to writing this book? My mission has been and continues to be *to help others improve their health, function, self-esteem, and overall well-being.* Life has been very good and very interesting to me, and there's still a sense of "I wish I knew then what I know now." Knowledge is power! By sharing my knowledge and experiences, along with stories about the challenges and successes of other health care providers, this book offers strategies for greater personal insight and awareness.

From this awareness, you empower yourself with better self-understanding, you can make choices that support yourself, and you can enjoy greater wellness.

Whether you are struggling to get through each day or you're thriving, *this book is for you!* Whether you are in training to become a health care provider, you are retired from health care services, or you're someplace in between, *this book is for you!* Regardless of whether you are a nurse, dentist, physician, therapist, assistant, mid-level provider, home health care aide, or any other health care provider, or you are caring for a parent, partner, or child with special health needs, *this book is for you!*

What can you expect from these pages? Each chapter covers a different aspect of wellness and includes exercises and techniques for self-awareness, self-care, and self-regulation. You can share these practices with your patients from a more holistic perspective so that they, too, might enjoy greater wellness. After each topic, the "Points to Ponder" sections give you the opportunity to reflect and explore different strategies and options. Chapter 8 includes links to yoga classes as well as still photos and guidance for practicing at your own pace, any time and any place. Regardless of your current situation, *you can improve your health, function, self-esteem, and overall well-being.*

1

UNEXPECTED GIFTS

How I literally imploded . . .

When I was 38 years old, I was bleeding to death internally.

I didn't realize it at the time, but that was a priceless opportunity.

At 38, my life was in pretty good order, or so I thought. I was contentedly married with a beautiful five-year-old daughter and sweet three-year-old son. We had a lovely home, close-knit family and friends, and everything we needed. My husband's work was providing a comfortable living for us. My career as a dentist was rising, so much so, in fact, that my business partner and I were planning major renovations and large technology and equipment purchases. The only problem was that, for the previous several years, my life had been so busy with maintaining my profession while still being a present mommy, and my space-sharing business partner had so many of his own busy-ness issues, that he and I had all but stopped communicating.

My business partner scheduled his vacations so that he could close his operatories for major demolition and construction, while I attempted to keep my office doors open, seeing patients despite the noise. (In actuality, the office was clean and disinfected. Construction areas had been sealed off with plastic and we had adequate ventilation and air filtration.) On several occasions I had to excuse myself from patients because I was coughing (on the dust, I told myself) and setting off asthma attacks. A couple of puffs of an albuterol inhaler and a glass of water later, I'd be back at the chair, performing microsurgery on anxious patients.

I'd stew in my anger and frustration, mentally cursing my partner for being so rude and inconsiderate as to schedule the work while I was seeing patients, but I never truly communicated with him about it. Then at the end of the day I'd drive more than half an hour home, stopping at daycare to pick up the kids before starting the evening routine of making supper, doing laundry, and squeezing in quality time with the kids before bath, books, and bedtime. Then it was back to the kitchen to clean up and pack lunches for the next day.

Talking with my husband was mostly relegated to our weekend date night, when we could find a babysitter. I was just too tired at night to talk. But everything was humming along as it should. Until it didn't.

One Sunday morning, my husband had just returned from being away on a multi-day trip. We didn't really get that much time together and we thought, well, maybe we can just plunk the kids in front of an educational video for 20 minutes and steal some alone time in our bedroom. Sneaking away like a couple of teenagers, we crept into bed and got reacquainted. Except, for some reason, things were really painful—like a stabbing sensation followed by a hot rush inside of me—and I just couldn't continue being intimate.

This first-ever occurrence was both disappointing and perplexing, but we chalked it up to a "fluke" and went about our day as a family, going for an autumn walk, catching flying leaves. By evening, I was feeling worse, really bloated, and I decided to go for a jog before dinner, hoping the movement would help me feel lighter. It didn't, and I felt rather lousy, as if my groin was splitting in half, like in the latter stages of pregnancy. Not one to take much medication and having a high pain threshold, I just went to bed shortly after the children were tucked in for the night. I decided that if I still felt bad when I awoke Monday morning, I might call my physician.

I fell asleep okay, and then I woke in the wee hours with a tremendous amount of pain. I was accustomed to getting up once at night to use the bathroom before falling back to sleep, so I got up and went. Only trouble was, I couldn't get back to bed. I found myself on the cold bathroom floor, unable to lift my body up even to crawl back to bed. I called out to my husband, "I need you." Thankfully, he heard me and sleepily came to see what was the matter. As he lifted me up to help me back to bed, I immediately sank to the floor like a sack of cement and proceeded to convulse for I don't know how long before I found stillness on my back.

My husband, incredulous and confused, was like "What the f*#@ just happened?"

At the moment, I didn't know. I only knew that I felt much better lying still on the cool floor. We decided that something was definitely not right with me, and weren't sure whether I'd had a small seizure or not. With the children in bed, my husband couldn't leave them alone to take me to the emergency room, so he called 911 for medical help.

When the ambulance crew arrived in a matter of minutes, they checked me out. I was still on the floor, but alert and oriented. They determined that I had probably not had a seizure, just merely fainted, and asked if I still wanted to go to the hospital. We were like "Hello? Yes!!" So off I went alone, on a stretcher into an ambulance with lights and siren on (even though I had asked for a silent ride!) in the middle of the night.

Once at the hospital, a male nurse and a female emergency medicine medical doctor examined me. They concluded that I had PMS, even though I told them I was around mid-cycle, and gave me Ibuprofen. They said that if I didn't feel better in a couple of days I should consult my physician. No need for an ob-gyn consult. No need for a noninvasive ultrasound. Just go home. Basically, the message was, "You're a bit hysterical, lady."

I was exhausted, I felt unheard, and now I felt embarrassed for seeking care—for actually calling 911 and coming to the emergency department by ambulance. I called my husband to come pick me up. Since we lived just minutes from the hospital, he showed up quickly, with the kids sleepy in their car seats, still in their pajamas, and I walked out of that place as quickly as I could, knowing in my heart that something was wrong and that these people were not going to believe me or help me.

Once we got home, I took a shower and got our daughter ready for school. My husband prepared for a busy Monday at his office, and we agreed that I should see my ob-gyn as soon as they opened. With our three-year-old in tow, I drove to the office. I implored the receptionist, "Can someone please see me? There's something wrong. I feel like I'm splitting in half and three months pregnant." They could fit me into the schedule mid-morning, so I brought my son to a nearby park and hoisted him onto the swings to entertain him for a while.

When I returned to the office, I met a doctor I'd never seen before. She performed a brief exam, and declared, "Honey, you're not okay." I exhaled, oddly relieved at being told that there was something wrong with me. Finally, someone believed me! Unfortunately, their ultrasound equipment was malfunctioning, and I was asked to come back after lunch. In the meantime, I phoned my parents, who were able to come over and watch our son while I went back to the doctor.

This time, as she scanned me, she told me, "You're full of blood. You need surgery."

Not one to be overly dramatic, I was like "Okay, when?"

And she replied, "No. You need surgery *now*."

She arranged with the on-call doctor to meet me at the hospital to have surgery straight away. On the 25-minute drive, I called my husband to meet me at the hospital, I called my office and had them reschedule my patients who were scheduled for the following day, I called my parents to let them know what was going on, and I phoned a friend to watch the kids overnight and get them to school and daycare the next day.

Waiting for operating room time late on a Monday afternoon, I looked and felt as if I had become five months pregnant overnight—my abdomen was visibly distended with blood and bloat. I consented to have an ovary removed, as they thought I had a fallopian tube in torsion. To my embarrassment, the last thing I remember saying to the anesthesiologist was, "This feels like a martini. No, two martinis." Thank goodness I don't remember anything after that!

In post-op recovery, I learned that I had had a hemorrhagic ovarian cyst, which was cauterized, and they also drained a soda can's worth of blood. I got to keep all my parts. I stayed overnight at the hospital, returning home in the morning. Of course, I thought I could go to work, at least in a couple of days. But what I learned is that even laparoscopy can make for a rough recovery. Activities of daily living, like bathing and dressing myself and the kids, doing laundry and dishes, were all a challenge. Losing blood and sleep and undergoing anesthesia had been exhausting, not to mention that my hormones were in absolute turmoil, contributing to raging mood swings. I didn't feel anything like myself for over a week. And then it was time to pick up the pieces at home and to resume business as usual at work . . . but not exactly.

Being a firm believer that everything happens for some reason, I feel that there are always lessons to be learned.

There are always lessons to be learned.

In fact, this was not my first brush with my own mortality, and I have learned to look for the gifts in trauma and tragedy. *This was a priceless opportunity—an unexpected gift—if only I would pay attention.* I reflected long and hard. What if I hadn't listened to my own body and advocated for myself? I could have died or minimally been hospitalized if I had listened to the advice I was given at the emergency department in the first hospital.

If I had suddenly died, how would I feel (before my final breath, obviously!) about my life thus far? I was a great dentist. I was a good daughter, sister, and friend. I was a wonderful mommy. My relationship with my husband? That could have used more attention. And myself? I was always putting everyone's needs ahead of my own—the children, my husband, the practice, my parents. Why did this happen?

It was an opportunity to reset, to check my priorities, and to realize what areas of my life needed more time and caring, including my relationship with myself.

While it would be a nice ending to the story to say that I learned my lessons and lived happily ever after, sometimes learning can be slow and incremental! I believe we are all works in progress, and I continue to develop and evolve by using these practices and perspectives. Consider for yourself a different approach to life and work challenges. We all have the capacity to learn, grow, and improve on a daily basis in order to live a life of greater wellness and joy.

2

WORK-LIFE BALANCE AND SELF-AWARENESS — KEYS TO ACHIEVING BLISS, NOT BURNOUT

Bliss Defined:

Noun: perfect happiness; great joy

Burnout Defined:

Noun: physical or mental collapse caused by overwork or stress

Dynamic Balance

Bliss, Not Burnout. Is bliss even attainable? Practically speaking, it's obviously neither realistic nor desirable to be happy all the time. Bitter balances sweet, clouds and rain balance sunshine. Without one we cannot appreciate the other. Challenges and stress are simply part of life. My personal aim is to experience more moments of joy, inspiration, and upliftment, so that I may lift others in the process as well. As John F. Kennedy said, "A rising tide lifts all ships." Certainly, burnout is not the goal. Wherein lies the balance?

It's been said that the concept of "work-life balance" is a myth. If we're thinking of the traditional balance scale, it's a rare and fleeting moment when our work life and our personal life are in perfect equilibrium. Life itself is not static; it's not like your car's cruise control where you can basically "set it and forget it." Some have likened balance to that of a mobile, where multiple pieces are hanging from a common source, and when just one of those pieces shifts into motion, or becomes heavier or lighter, the entire systemic balance shifts.

Having spent a great deal of time in physical therapy as a patient myself, it occurred to me that balance in life is actually very dynamic—kind of like balancing on a yoga or BOSU ball!

Dynamic balance requires you to enlist various muscle groups simultaneously and in varying intensities in order to balance yourself. After I had planned foot surgery that included fusion of my big toe, I needed to relearn how to use all the small muscles in my foot and ankle in new and different ways in order to achieve balance again. Much of that practice utilized standing on a BOSU ball while engaging in strength training and balancing exercises.

Likewise, in yoga we practice one-legged balancing postures to increase lower body and core strength, as well as overall balance. This kind of dynamic balance requires adjusting the alignment of your bones over your joints, making continuous micro-adjustments to the supporting muscles. It also necessitates centering in oneself, both body and mind, and becomes easier when you bring your awareness back to your breath while focusing on a focal point (Dristi, also spelled Drishti as seen in other references)[1]. As it turns out, life is much that way. There are many moving parts and pieces. When you come back to center (being grounded and congruent with your purpose) while mindfully drawing your attention to your breath, you are better able to make the continuous little adjustments that are necessary to stay on target and balanced.

You may be thinking that this concept of dynamic balance requires a great deal of self-awareness in order to make the continuous sequence of tiny adjustments, and you are correct! With all the demands and distractions in today's world—the nonstop barrage of billboards and messages and media and notifications—it's easy to become disembodied from your authentic self. In order to begin living life more fully and healthfully, you need to become reacquainted with yourself. Remember, *you already have all the tools and resources that you need,* basically for free or at very little cost, to access your higher level of living and being. You don't need someone or something to fix you. With just a subtle shift in perspective, you'll be able to consider the same old issues in a fresh, new light. Possibilities will open right before your eyes. While opportunities may have been there all along, you may not have seen them before. Much like getting corrective lenses, you'll have clearer vision in all dimensions. Give yourself the gift of renewed life, a second chance without the ambulance ride to the emergency department. You might even save your own life!

Self-Aware, Self-Care, and Self-Compassion

Self-Aware

I found myself writing at the kitchen table on a rainy Saturday morning. Except for the dogs, the rest of the house was asleep. I was struck with the realization that, in

---

[1]   Since Sanskrit language uses characters and diacritical marks that do not have a one-to-one exact correspondence to the English/Romance languages alphabet, pronunciation can vary and you may notice that many Sanskrit words have more than one meaning/spelling. For the sake of this work and to eliminate confusion, while I use Dristi, both Dristi and Drishti are correct.

addition to being nourishing and hydrating and cleansing, rain is also an invitation to be soothed, to be grounded, to "go inside" and be in touch with whatever resides there. Going inside yourself is the means to being self-aware. And being self-aware is an absolute prerequisite to practicing self-care. After all, if you aren't in touch with yourself, with what you're feeling physically and emotionally, how can you know what you need to do to care for yourself?

If you're feeling tired, depleted, or just plain unmotivated, what do you need? Perhaps you're dehydrated. When was the last time you "watered" yourself—literally drank a glass of water? Or you get home from work and head straight for a bag of chips to crunch and a bottle of beer to wash it down to "relax" after a long day. Perhaps a short walk around the neighborhood would suit you better first. Are the "crunchy munchies" your body's way of letting off aggression or restless energy? Do you need to use your mouth to express yourself or let off some built-up "steam" or tension from your day? Might chatting with a neighbor, throwing a ball for your dog to retrieve, or pulling a few rogue weeds from your garden serve you better?

> "You've got to deal with the feel in order to heal."

Notice your body talking to you: is your gut tied up in knots? Your belly could be telling you that you're frustrated with not moving forward with your ambitions or desires the way you'd like to. "Great," you say, "I already knew I hated my job and I'm not exactly 'living the dream.' How does dwelling on that help me?" Dwelling on feelings, whether they be feelings of "I'm not good enough," "I feel stuck," or any other emotions, is not the goal here. *Feeling* them—acknowledging them without judgment, being aware of them in the first place—*is* the goal. Because *you've got to feel to heal!* You absolutely will *not* progress forward if you don't even know where you are to begin with. I'm not advocating Freudian psychotherapy here. I'm simply saying that *your feelings have feelings too.*

Feelings need to be acknowledged and recognized. Like small children, feelings need to be seen, held, and heard. They *don't* need to be judged! How's that for releasing any guilt or shame? Feelings are just that: feelings. They are called feelings because you feel them viscerally in your physical body, not just in your mind. And even if you don't particularly like the way you're feeling, you'll probably continue to feel that way, over and over again, until you start listening to your feelings, become fully present with them, and accept them without judgment. This unconditional acceptance of your feelings, of your*self*, is the first step toward healing yourself and the first step in moving forward and toward where you'd rather be and what you'd rather be feeling.

"It's no big deal," you say, "Anyone would be pissed off if they had so much responsibility at work that they couldn't possibly get everything done to the boss's satisfaction, and then drove home through rush-hour traffic to be greeted by a mailbox full of bills and a cat who'd thrown up hairballs on the carpet."

This is true, most people would feel irritated, and these are not earth-shattering events that have caused you to feel annoyed. But stuffing those feelings into your core, either by eating or drinking, escaping into mindless television, or running head-on into the next list of chores and frustrations, does *not* allow you to acknowledge yourself so you can release toxic energy and move on with your evening.

Maybe you call a friend and take turns sharing in each other's day. Maybe you schedule time for a yoga or other exercise class on the way home from work. No time? No money? No problem! Take six minutes to go into your bedroom or bathroom—or even to stop before you get home and use your smartphone—to listen to a free online meditation. Or borrow a free download from your local public library. The short-term ease of excuses can outweigh the long-term ease of accessing a free download for six minutes.

I know, I've been there. I would rush to get to daycare before it closed and I didn't think I had a second for myself. Because as soon as I got home, I had to breastfeed my baby, make some semblance of a healthy dinner for my preschooler (who also needed and deserved time with mommy), start the laundry, clean up messes, spend time with family, bathe the children and read with them before bed, then head back to the kitchen to prepare everyone's bags and lunches for the next day. Eventually, I'd make it to the shower and not much else before collapsing in bed. Then I'd be up in the night with a crying baby, wake up to an alarm feeling unrested, get everyone up and ready for the day, drop the kids off at daycare and head off to work to do it all over again.

And I did. For a long time. Because I'm Superwoman and I'm strong and I can do it all. And I could, until I couldn't. Until I was so stressed and exhausted and ignoring my body's warning signs (increasing incidences of asthma, difficulty breathing at work, moodiness) that I finally ended up imploding with life-threatening internal bleeding, which I still ignored and pushed through for a day. As a survivor of my own self-neglect, I'm here to say that you cannot afford *not* to be self-aware. Your well-being, your mere existence, and your longevity depend upon your being self-aware. Once you get reacquainted with yourself, you can take the next step of taking care of yourself, and I promise you will be so much more effective and efficient than if you continued being busy being busy.

Self-Care:

The #1 Best Stress-Busting Strategy

Just when you feel that you're at your wits' end, that you absolutely have *no time* to _____ (fill in the blank: eat properly, exercise, get a good night's rest, make time for people and activities you enjoy), that is *precisely* the time that you *must* slow down and make time for *you*. I know, I know, you don't even have time to go to the bathroom without being interrupted. You're so busy that you can't think straight and frequently go in circles. You couldn't possibly press the "pause" button for even 30 minutes to care for yourself. You have so many people and things that you are responsible for—things that no one could possibly understand or relate to.

Oh, really? Do you honestly think you are so unique and special that neither I nor anyone else would or could ever relate to or understand your situation? Well, that is bullshit. In fact, it's a big old lie—a story that you're telling yourself, and it doesn't serve you. I'm here to call you out and make the argument that:

The #1 thing you can do to improve and preserve your positive health is to slow down, get reacquainted with yourself (see previous section on self-awareness), and practice self-care and self-compassion.

Before you can be aware of others, care for others, and be compassionate toward others, you first need to practice these things for your*self*.

So what does that mean? And, practically speaking, how do you begin? And even if you are taking fairly good care of yourself, what would it feel like to take even *better* care of yourself—even just 5 to 10 percent better—by eating healthier, sleeping restfully, and exercising in ways that consistently boost your mental/cognitive/emotional abilities?

Whoa! By now you're thinking that I've had too much caffeine, and you might be partly correct, but not entirely.

One Sunday afternoon I was sitting and chatting with my husband about practicing my own self-care, and he said, "What's that?"

And I'm like, "Exactly! Who makes time for themselves in a meaningful way?" And then I took a breath and realized that he was being sincere. Most of us were never taught to take care of ourselves. Not beyond the basic eat-your-veggies and brush-your-teeth-before-bed kinds of things. So what am I *actually* talking about? I'm talking about checking in with yourself throughout the day—truly pausing and asking yourself what and how you're feeling mentally, physically, and emotionally.

One great way to do that is to journal. Just get it all out on paper in a virtual free-flow of thoughts early in the morning, before you set about the rest of your day. You could certainly add specific exercises or routines to the process, but if you're not in the habit of journaling, here are a few prompts to get you started:

Right now I feel _____ (happy, sad, angry, stressed, etc.).

In my physical body I'm noticing _____ (tension [where?], temperature, movement, fullness, lightness, bubbling/rumbling, etc.).

The quality of my thoughts is _____ (slow, racing, random, worrying about the future, perseverating about something that has passed, etc.).

My overall energy feels _____ (frenetic, lethargic, focused, grounded, scattered, positive, doubtful, depressed, enthusiastic, etc.).

Once you have a better sense of your starting point (=self-awareness), you can move on to the next question, which is:

"What do I need right now?"

What does your body need? Maybe water for hydration, protein for strength, fruits and vegetables for energy and vitamins, fats for lubrication and sustenance. Does your body crave movement, and if so, does it want to move energetically/aerobically? Perhaps you'd benefit from going for a jog outdoors or freestyle dancing in your bedroom! Does your body need rest? Perhaps this is not the day to rise at 5:00 a.m. to go to the gym. If your body truly needs rest, it might serve you best to rest in and consider going for a walk at lunchtime or at the end of your day.

What about your thoughts? Are they sluggish and depressed? Try focusing on your breathing, taking complete breaths that start with the abdomen expanding and then filling your core up to your chest completely before exhaling in a one-to-one ratio (equal length inhales and exhales).

Are your thoughts frenetic, scattered, or anxious over future possibilities? Again, focus on complete breaths, and gradually increase the length of your exhales, as if you are ever-so-slowly releasing air from a balloon and don't want it to explode into spirals all over the room. Work up to exhales that are at least twice as long as your inhales if you can do so without straining. Another option here is alternate nostril breathing (Nadi Shodhana or Anuloma Viloma). I'll review these techniques in more depth a little further on. (How's that for a teaser?!)

Next, consider where you want to go/be and what you want to do. Do you have a huge presentation today that requires you to look and feel your most confident, energetic, and focused self? What would prepare you to be in that space? Again, check in with yourself. Do you need rest, like a 20-minute power nap or a restorative yoga posture with your eyes closed and the lights dimmed? Do you need to rev up your energy quickly? Maybe some jumping jacks or Kapalabhati energizing breathwork (again, more to come!) would clear your mind and energize your body. Do you need physical stamina? What type of breakfast would sustain you the most? Or do you need to keep light and alert, eating just light meals of lean protein and vegetables? Is your head tight with tension? If so, when was the last time you hydrated with water? Perhaps a little self-massage would relieve some tightness around the temples, jaw, and neck.

The main idea here is to check in with yourself, acknowledge exactly the way you are without judging it, and then consider where you want to be. Once you've acknowledged where you are and are more self-aware in the moment, there is no reason for you to wallow or stay stuck there if it's not where you want to be. The important thing is to recognize where you're starting from, because if you just soldier on and plow into the next activity, there's a good chance that you'll be plowing yourself into the ground from not taking care of your own needs.

Maybe you consider what lies ahead in your day and you say to yourself, "This is simply too much. There's no way I can accomplish all of these things to the best of my abilities and still come out intact at the end of the day." Well, if that's your self-aware realization, congratulations to you! That is a most magnificent thing to be cognizant of, and when you recognize this at the beginning of your day (because you're journaling and getting your head together, right?), then you can course-correct.

Maybe you say no to the work lunch meeting, meet by phone to save some of your lunch break time for yourself, postpone the meeting to a more suitable day, or cancel it altogether! Or take some of those to-dos off your list and move them to another day. Is it critical that you dust the knickknacks today? Or will the dust be there waiting for you in a couple of days when you have more time for that chore? Will paying the bills today give you peace of mind, or will paying them tomorrow work just as well? In the end, it's up to you—it's your choice!

Self-Compassion

It has been said that self-compassion is simply giving yourself the same kindness that you would offer to others. It sounds so simple, and yet why do we find it so hard to put into practice at times? Whenever you hear that nagging, niggling, self-deprecating, negative inner voice talking, you are *not* practicing self-compassion. Whenever you tell yourself what you cannot do, what isn't good enough (or smart enough or good-looking enough or whatever enough), remind yourself to be just a little more kind.

In many ways, our minds are not that complex; what we think, we can believe. When you tell yourself something, whether it be positive or negative, accurate or untrue, your subconscious takes it as a matter of fact. So why would you tell yourself that you're stupid or ugly or out of shape or lazy or any other unflattering thing? Why not try the opposite? How would it be to look in the mirror and tell yourself what a "winner" you are, or any of a host of other positive affirmations? Even if it's something you aspire to be but don't feel is true at this moment, how would it serve you to speak/reinforce these ideas as if they were already true?

It may seem trivial, but for most of my life I've struggled with a negative body image. I always felt like my legs were too short and stubby and chubby. No matter how hard I tried lifting weights and aerobic exercise and dieting, I still had thick thighs that felt unattractive to me.

One day when I was 30-something, I had an "aha" moment! Why did I persist in fighting with reality? I would never have long and lanky legs, and that was absolutely fine. I began to think about my physical self differently—to appreciate all that my legs could do: carry me around, dance, ski, cycle, and more. And I developed a softness with my thoughts around my legs–compassion, self-compassion. I began to love the things that my body could do, the experiences that were available because I have healthy legs.

And a truly interesting thing happened. As my attitude and perspective changed, the way I perceived myself evolved as well. My physical body morphed and became more attractive to me, simply because I'd changed to a compassionate approach. Did anything objectively change? Probably not, but since reality is subject to individual interpretation, my reality shifted, my experience of life transformed, and I enjoyed greater peace and well-being.

What could life be like for you if you cared for yourself as compassionately as you would care for a beloved friend or family member? As a health care provider, you are hard-wired to care for others day in and day out. But you can't have an endless abundance of caring and compassion if you don't restore your own reserves. It would be like trying to drive cross-country without ever stopping to refuel your gas tank—you'd never make it! Think about your favorite electronic devices, perhaps your smartphone or computer. Every day you make sure that these devices are recharged so that their battery is fully renewed and ready for the next day. Do the same for yourself!

When you are self-aware, you can practice self-care, and when you practice self-care, you become self-compassionate. Does this all seem a bit simplistic or even selfish? On the contrary, these practices enable you to become more aware, more caring, and more compassionate toward not only your patients, but also your family, friends, and others in your personal life and community.

Again, to be intentionally repetitive, self-awareness, self-care, and self compassion are essential to your well-being! In Chapter 3, I'll introduce some simple tools that you can begin to use immediately, not only to increase your self-awareness, but also to improve your self-care by identifying your needs from an elemental perspective.

Points to Ponder

- How do you currently practice self-care?
- With greater self-awareness, what do you need in order to enjoy even greater well-being? (More sleep? Better nutrition? Regular massages? Help with housework? An exercise buddy? Personal coach? Talk therapy?) Calendar your next steps to prioritize yourself!

3

PHYSICAL AND MENTAL HEALTH

(Spoiler Alert: They're Interrelated!)

Wellness for health care providers might seem obvious, and yet great health is not automatically bestowed upon us once we receive our degree/certification/license or when we begin caring for our first patients. There are plenty of examples of physicians who don't follow their own advice on nutrition and exercise. While many health care providers may know better, they simply don't have the time or energy to properly care for themselves.

In a recent survey of health care providers, 20 percent stated that their work contributed to physical pain (shoulder, neck, back, hips, and joint and foot pain) from standing for much of their work day.[2] Regarding maintaining healthy body weight, 19 percent felt that working in health care had contributed to weight problems; 3 percent lost weight due to stress; and 16 percent attributed unhealthy weight gain to the demands of working in health care—not enough time to eat healthy meals while working (substituting fast/processed/convenience foods) and not enough time/energy to exercise regularly. What this means to us as health care providers as a group is that, with greater awareness, we can take steps toward better self-care and prioritize our own health.

Regarding mental health, one third of those surveyed felt that working with the demands of health care contributed to stress/frustration, worry/anxiety, loss of ambition, depression, and mental exhaustion. As Jason, a retired medical doctor,

---

[2]   In 2023, I surveyed and interviewed hundreds of health care providers from all regions of the United States regarding their experiences working in health care and their self-perceived wellness. Unless otherwise stated, the stories and statistics cited are derived from the analysis of my aggregate findings.

shared, "Being a physician made me physically and mentally ill for years. Now that I'm out of the system, I finally feel healthy."[3]

This is not a call for health care providers to exit the workforce—the pandemic already took a hefty toll on the health care system workforce. Rather, Jason speaks for many of us and rings out a cry for help. Health care providers need to feel healthy and supported. You deserve better work-life balance so that you can care for yourself, which also allows you to better care for your patients.

In the same survey, only 28 percent felt that their work as a health care provider had positively impacted their health. One common reason was feeling motivated to improve their health. As Susan, an office manager, put it, "When you see patients, this prompts you to take better care of your health."

Jeremy, an adult psychiatric advanced practice registered nurse (APRN), shared that his work "motivates me to do some of the things that I tell my patients to do."[4]

Another respondent, a primary care provider, stated, "I feel better physically and mentally because I feel like I have a purpose in life." Other health care providers agreed that their work in health care gave them satisfaction, joy, and the reward of being able to help other people.

So what can we learn from those who fare well? What are they doing differently, and how can those who are at risk of *Burnout* turn their situation into *Bliss?*

Exercise

Exercise is critical for both physical and mental well-being. You already know that. In fact, you probably recommend regular exercise to your patients. You probably also know that making the time and effort to exercise yourself can be a logistical and energetic challenge. When you're feeling completely depleted at the end of the day, you might be inclined to escape rather than engage in exercise. James, an embalmer/funeral director, admits, "I feel like my work has brought me anxiety because I'm constantly thinking about death and the ways that people are dying. I've not been able to manage the stress or maintain a healthy weight for a while. Instead, I tend to use unhealthy habits to cope, including cigarettes and drinking."

Natasha, a medical assistant in dermatology, admits that "working in health care has brought me stress at times. I used to drink alcohol as a stress reliever, but stopped

---

[3]   All names of the health care providers who participated in my interviews/surveys/research have been changed to protect their privacy and any potential Health Insurance Portability and Accountability Act (HIPAA) conflict.

[4]   My research revealed regional differences in credentials for health care providers with similar responsibilities. For example, Advanced Practice Registered Nurse is a common designation for a midlevel provider on the east coast.

that and started **working out** and going to bed earlier for **more rest**. Curing skin cancer has brought me a sense of **joy** to help people."

Jennifer, a psychotherapist, notes that her work "contributes to anxiety, but has also brought greater joy and purpose in life. **Walking, talk therapy,** and **talking with friends** have been helpful strategies, even though my stress remains."

This raises an important point. The idea of *Bliss, Not Burnout* does not suggest that the stressors in your life will necessarily change appreciably, but that what can change is how you respond to those stressors, how you manage your reactions, and how you take care of yourself.

While 25 percent of survey respondents cited **working out/lifting weights/ going to the gym** as an exercise strategy that helped them to manage stress, more than 12 percent of respondents expressed that **walking** and/or **jogging** were working for them. In particular, walking is readily available to almost everyone. Walking does not require special clothing, equipment, or expensive memberships. Walking can be done for hours, such as a hike, or for only minutes at a time before or after work, or during a meal break.

> What can change is how you respond to those stressors, how you manage your reactions, and how you take care of yourself.

Points to Ponder

- What does your current exercise regimen look like?
- Where might you incorporate just a bit more physical movement into your day? (for example, could you walk or ride a bicycle to work? Can you park your car further from the building? Might you choose to take the stairs instead of an elevator? Could you take time during a break to go for a walk, either indoors or preferably outdoors? Could you start your day with some energizing exercise and/or end your day with some relaxing stretches?) Calendar your exercise plans for the coming week!

■ ■ ■

Minibreaks: Mindfulness, Meditation, Breathing, and Prayer

As it turns out, self-awareness and self-regulation are key factors to stress management in the workplace and beyond. Sundar, a lab technician, feels that working in health care "has brought greater joy to me. I manage stress by **being relaxed** at my work." At times, this is easier said than done, and yet Sundar is talking about *intentionally* caring for himself by affirming how he approaches his day.

What does that look like? It could mean listening to calming music while working, or allowing a bit more time to care for yourself and to ready your body and mind before your work day. Journaling, meditation, stretching, walking, breathing, mindfulness—these are all tools and strategies that are free and available to you on a regular basis. "But I don't have time!" you scream. Exactly. *And* you don't have time *not* to take care of yourself. Precisely the moment when you feel you haven't a minute to spare is when you need to spare it the most.

It doesn't have to be huge. When I was single and before I had children, I wouldn't go to the gym unless I had at least 90 minutes to lift weights and do cardio workouts. After marriage and children, I realized I needed to be more creative and resourceful than that. Something is better than nothing. Waiting for the perfect conditions is the enemy of growth and improvement. When I studied with the Pankey Institute for postgraduate dental education, they would ask, "When are you going to _____ ?" (Fill in the blank with your uncomfortable change or elusive goal.)

For the "uninitiated" in the room, the response was usually along the lines of "Someday I'll get around to it."

Invariably, the instructor would pull out of his pocket a wooden token inscribed with the letters "TUIT" and hand it to the rookie dentist. "Here you go, a round TUIT." In other words, if not now, when? The same holds true for giving yourself time for work breaks and self-care.

It's possible to take **minibreaks** that reap big rewards with your wellness. If you're working at a desk, lab bench, or computer, you can set an alarm for every 50 to 55 minutes to remind yourself to get up, **stretch, get a drink of water, close your eyes,** or **use the restroom**. If you're working directly with patients, you can take a **mini-meditation** on your break—even 30 seconds of slow, **mindful breathing** makes a difference in getting you back into your body and in the present moment. Better yet, invite your patient to breathe with you—you'll both feel more calm, present, and relaxed! When you have a few or more minutes, take a stroll down the hall or outdoors to get a breath of fresh air and a change of scenery. It's guaranteed to give you a fresh perspective or at least a renewed energetic approach to your challenges.

> Waiting for the perfect conditions is the enemy of growth and improvement.

Mindfulness, meditation, breathing, and prayer were cited as being helpful coping mechanisms by 20 percent of health care providers surveyed. Amoke, a medical doctor, shared that "**Yoga, gardening, listening to music,** and going on **walks** work tremendously!"

With their emphasis on breathing with mindful movement, yoga, tai chi, and other martial arts can provide physical, mental, and energetic benefits. According to Jennifer Martin, PhD, clinical psychologist and president of the American Academy of Sleep Medicine, cognitive behavioral therapy for insomnia (CBT-I) is the first line of treatment for insomnia, *not* sleeping pills, sedatives, or other medications. It's estimated that CBT-I is effective for 75 percent of patients who are compliant with therapy. For the remaining 25 percent of patients, **yoga** and **tai chi** can help!

Gardening can be performed both mindfully and meditatively by experiencing the earth and plant life with all the senses in the present moment. **Listening to music** can affect your energy by lifting low spirits with energetic and inspirational tunes, and music can soothe frayed nerves with calmer melodies and instrumental pieces.

There can be a fine line between prayer and meditation. For some individuals, these are one and the same activity. I talk more about the definition of meditation in the section "Using the Five Great Elements" to increase self-awareness. In both prayer and meditation, there is connection with a higher power, universe, or community—a felt sense of a greater unifying energy—and this supports the human need for connection. Kristen Rogers reported on CNN's website in "The Psychological Benefits of Prayer: What Science Says about the Mind-Soul Connection" that "Prayer has been hard to study, but the research we do have shows that prayer can reduce feelings of isolation, anxiety, and fear."

She quoted Kevin Masters, a professor of clinical health psychology at the University of Colorado, Denver, who said, "We are now quite aware that psychological experiences are intimately associated with important physiological processes, including immune system functioning. To the extent that prayer can impact those psychological processes we have, potentially, naturalistic explanations for how prayer could impact health."

On a personal level, when I had a bicycling accident that resulted in a traumatic brain injury as a teenager, I received cards and flowers with notes wishing me a full and speedy recovery from people I had never met who were friends of my family and acquaintances. Each prayer and message, even the prayers that I never heard, gave me hope and strength. To this day when I hear sirens or pass the scene of an accident or emergency, I send up healing and wellness wishes for both the people who need emergency services as well as the first responders who are helping them. And for the nonspiritual, thinking good thoughts couldn't hurt, right?

Points to Ponder

- How might you incorporate more minibreaks into your day? Look at your calendar. Make a date with yourself.
- What daily activities could you perform more mindfully/meditatively by being more present in the moment? (Think: chopping vegetables, folding laundry, eating meals, etc.)
- How can you use the power of breathing to ground yourself and those around you? (Think: inviting patients, coworkers, friends, or family to take a

breath with you; taking a personal breathing break once every hour to clear your mind and body; practicing slow, steady, deep breathing while driving or commuting to work, etc.)

■ ■ ■

Hobbies, Reading, and Interests

More than 10 percent of health care providers surveyed cited some type of hobby as a useful and positive stress management strategy. Common interests included:

- Listening to music, singing, or playing a musical instrument
- Creating visual art by painting, drawing, sculpting, or even coloring
- Gardening or doing yard work
- Sewing/embroidery/knitting/crocheting
- Cooking or baking
- Playing games or solving puzzles

One of the beautiful things about the preceding activities is that they can be done alone or with others, or some combination thereof. Even reading can become a group activity when you join a book discussion group or share thoughts about an online article with a friend.

Leslie, a senior consultant in quality outcomes, describes their passion for raising butterflies: "Caring for caterpillars is time-consuming but gratifying. When a beautiful butterfly emerges from a chrysalis, it is wonderful."

Mihaly Csikszentmihalyi, psychologist and author of the *New York Times* best-selling book *Flow,* defines "flow" as a highly focused mental state conducive to productivity. Any activity in which we can lose our creative selves and attain this state of flow also has the potential to be meditative and mindful.

Retired psychiatrist Alan describes his hobbies and interests outside of work:

I greatly enjoy **reading** and learning about nonmedical topics, especially inspirational biographies of famous artists and their works. I love **bird and animal watching** in my yard and **learning** to identify them by sight and sound. I take care of the squirrels and birds in my yard. I built an extensive array of feeders—different colors and shapes with different kinds of seed for the local species of birds—on what can best be described as a "tree" (a metal "trunk" off of which I've hung "branches"). The overall concept was to make it sort of like a Christmas tree with bird feeders as "ornaments." I have special squirrel feeders in one of my real trees in the backyard. It has been therapeutic and rewarding.

Points to Ponder

- What hobbies and interests do you currently enjoy? Have you thought about learning something new? (Think: how to knit, a musical instrument, a new recipe, etc.). Novelty is stimulating and could help you stick with it! What interest has been simmering on the back burner, just waiting for you to turn up the heat and add some spices?
- What have you read lately? This includes online blogs and posts, books, magazine articles, and more. What topics inspire and delight you?
- What do you enjoy just for fun? How might you add a little more fun and newness to your routine?

■ ■ ■

Connection and Community

Sometimes working in health care can feel like you're isolated from the support of colleagues and even from friends and family. For many, working and living through a global pandemic exacerbated feelings of loneliness. Monique, a pharmacist, experienced stress as a concomitant of "depression and anxiety, being alienated from the community as a result of their poor response to COVID." Her path back to her purpose included medication (for her mood disorders), **working out, getting more sleep,** and **time with friends and family**.

Difficult work conditions pose serious challenges. Marisol, a certified nurse's aide, reflects on her isolation during the height of the pandemic:

> In skilled nursing facilities, you get to know your patients and their families on a very personal level. Every day is different on a rehab wing, trying to meet all the patients' needs in a timely manner. My goal has always been to go home feeling that I did the best I could caring for my patients.
>
> During COVID I became very anxious caring for COVID patients. Working short-staffed all the time, we had to do things we had never done before, having to put so many deceased patients in body bags. I felt very isolated from my friends and family because of what I did for work. Especially during those times, I tried to **start the day with a little exercise**. Throughout the day I'd practice some **deep breathing**, and at the end of the day I relaxed with my **hobbies** and a **prayer** before bed.

Working as part of a health care team can provide its own sense of camaraderie and **community**. Jess describes the impacts of working as a registered nurse and patient services manager for nearly 15 years:

While I have a high sense of purpose in my work, I've felt fairly dissatisfied over the past six months. I feel like both my physical and mental health are only about average. Stress and tension at work typically run very high, and by the end of the work day, I'm fatigued. In nursing school, we were taught how to take care of others, but we weren't trained on how to manage stress and practice self-care.

My ideal work day involves being able to be productive without having to deal with constant complaints and conflict amongst coworkers. I aim to be proactive rather than reactive/putting out fires all day. Being able to wrap up work on time so I can get home to my family makes my time being at work so much more enjoyable—work-life balance is healthier.

On the other hand, juggling the demands of childcare, finances, and employees who stir up drama is draining. At a recent staff meeting in front of the vice president of our service line, certain staff members directly challenged me. Instead of getting drawn into their drama, I was able to redirect and restate our objectives. After the meeting, the VP told me privately that my response was perfect and I handled the situation very well.

At this point, I benefit from **talk therapy** and **medication management**. If it's been a particularly difficult day, I enjoy a glass of wine. Spending time at home with **family** is recharging, and spending time **gardening** and **being outdoors** is essential—I find it even more effective than talk therapy! At the end of the day, I feel grateful to have a positive impact on others' lives. It's also rewarding to improve what often feels like a broken (health care) system.

Regarding the impact of my work as a health care provider on my relationships, there's a very special and unique bond that forms from being in the trenches with other nurses. For example, working during COVID or in a critical care environment, you learn to really lean on those around you for support, and that bond never goes away. It's a lifelong understanding that you've seen the worst together and had each other's back during it. For personal relationships, you realize it's harder to relate to certain people, and some of those friendships fade.

Points to Ponder

- Who are your "people"? How often do you connect with them? Whether you consider yourself to be an extrovert or an introvert, humans have a basic need for connection and community. We were designed to thrive as social beings, not hermits.
- How might you increase your sense of connection to your loved ones on a daily basis? (Think: planned time together, phone conversation, checking in with a text, etc.)
- How might you increase your connection to your community? (Think: spending time with coworkers outside of work; volunteering in your community; participating in a class/discussion group/musical group/place of worship, etc.)

■ ■ ■

Ergonomics

No matter your role as a health care provider, ergonomics can be an issue. Pediatricians frequently meet their patients on a table, the floor, in their parent's lap—wherever they can reach them! Other situations present unique physical challenges. One young emergency medical technician found herself donning a fireman's helmet and jacket while huddling under a blanket with an overdosed patient who had rolled herself and her vehicle into a ditch. They needed to have the car literally cut open, raining metal and glass everywhere, in order to remove the patient and transport her to hospital emergency services. Certified nurses' aids are continuously lifting, bending, and stretching in order to bathe, dress, feed, and transport their patients. Nurses are all too familiar with the copious amounts of documentation that is necessary in health care today, and documentation necessitates a considerable amount of time hunched and contracted over a computer screen.

Those who work as a nurse, aide, medical or dental assistant, physician, physician associate, or in so many other health care provider roles may find themselves bending, leaning, stretching, and otherwise twisting to help a patient who is compromised. It's what we do, to the best of our abilities. But it comes at a cost. Chronically poor posture contributes to muscle, neck, and back strain. In addition to repetitive motion injuries, many in health care are prone to sustained static postural injuries and nerve compression. Dentists, hygienists, dental assistants, surgeons, and others can develop frozen shoulder (adhesive capsulitis) if they don't *counteract the effects with balancing stretches.*

Chiropractors manipulate the body's alignment to relieve pain, improve function, and help the body to heal itself. In my role as a dentist, I'm concerned with aligning my patients' teeth and jaws, so why shouldn't I be concerned with aligning my own body? As a certified yoga instructor, I teach the importance of "stacking" joints to align them to support bearing weight. For instance, when simply standing, one should have hips over knees over ankles.

Despite the physical demands of being a health care provider, there is much that we can do to keep ourselves well *once we have greater awareness.* Taking even just 10 or 15 minutes in the morning to stretch, mobilize, and lubricate the major joints of the shoulders, spine, wrists, hips, and ankles can go a long way in preparing your body for the day and preventing injuries.

Consider yourself preparing for a 5K fun run or walk. Would you just step out and start running, or would you stretch a bit before you began? If you did just start out "cold" from the starting line, that might work for you, but you would be more prone to twisting an ankle or straining your hamstrings. When you stretch ahead of time, your muscles are warmer, more responsive, and ready to perform optimally. Whether at work or in your personal life, wouldn't you want this for yourself every day?

Perhaps you're already practicing a robust fitness program, and if so, kudos to you! But if you find yourself too rushed in the morning to even consider exercise (or you have young children or pets to care for, or a long commute, or you can't afford a gym membership, or you don't own the right fitness gear, or a million other reasons why you don't stretch), you can set your alarm for just 10 minutes earlier and try the exercises in Chapter 8 to prime yourself for the day.

4

INTEGRATIVE MEDICINE —
THE ABCS OF ELEMENTAL-WELLNESS:
"A" IS FOR ĀYURVEDA

"A" Is for Āyurveda, Attitude, and Appreciation

What Exactly Is Elemental-Wellness, and What Are Its Origins?

I'm so glad you asked! Elemental-Wellness is a unique version of integrative medicine that derives from Western (allopathic) medicine, yoga, and āyurveda (traditional Indian medicine), sleep medicine, and breathing (pranayama) that provides tools for greater self-awareness, self-care, and thereby greater well-being. As a health care provider, you already know a great deal about health and wellness, and you're probably spending a tremendous amount of time and energy in helping others, particularly your patients, to be well.

In one sense, you can stop reading right now—perhaps what I have to say isn't a total newsflash for you. But on the other hand, based on the fact that you have read this far, perhaps you have at least some curiosity as to how you can live your best life. You continue to glean information on multiple levels: nutrition, sleep, physical movement to better align your physical body, and practices to support mental health. Here you continue to decrease detrimental stress and burnout while simultaneously increasing your joy and overall wellness and well-being.

No matter what your circumstances, who wouldn't want more of that? And the beautiful thing is that you can access these offerings for free, *and* you already have the tools you need to live your life with greater ease, wellness, and joy—you just might need a little guidance, permission, or reminders to access your innate wellness.

Elemental-Wellness derives from the Five Great Elements (Panča Maha Bhutas, also spelled Pancha Maha Bhutas) of Āyurveda as the basis for understanding all of life, and particularly oneself, in order to make proactive choices that are in alignment with greater well-being. And when you invariably stray off course, Elemental-Wellness gives you both an understanding of your tendencies and practical strategies to get back on track again. Elemental-Wellness is exactly what it says: it is both elemental, or simple, and yet profound at the same time!

Welcome to Elemental-Wellness! Let's dive in . . .

Complement Defined:

Noun: A thing that completes or brings to perfection
Verb: To add to (something) in a way that enhances or improves it; make perfect

"A" is for Āyurveda

An Introduction

The Five Great Elements

One of the beauties of Elemental-Wellness is that it complements one's existing knowledge base and belief system(s), providing another lens or perspective through which to view life. For example, in the past I might have viewed someone exhibiting anger, rudeness, and road rage as being a nasty, unreasonable idiot. Sounds a bit *judgmental*, doesn't it?

> Elemental-Wellness is exactly what it says: it is both elemental, or simple, and yet profound at the same time!

Through the vision of Elemental-Wellness, however, I can *observe* that this same person is experiencing a pitta imbalance caused by an excess of the Fire Element (more on these terms later). "That's nice," you say, "but what exactly does that mean and how does it make the situation better?" Great questions! It means that I can observe and choose my response, instead of just defaulting to a knee-jerk reaction, and now I have a better understanding of how to choose how I respond. Instead of getting all hot and bothered, perhaps yelling at the person or upsetting myself, I realize that in order to take care of myself, I need to balance his/her excess Fire with extra Earth (grounding, stability, strength) and Space (levity, coolness, higher understanding). More on this in a little while . . .

In the Introduction, I alluded to the ancient wisdom of āyurveda, the thousands-of-years-old tradition of Indian Medicine that is still practiced today. In Sanskrit, the word "āyur" means "life" and "veda" means "knowledge." Together this means "life wisdom or knowledge," and more commonly it's known as the sister science to yoga.

In fact, yoga and āyurveda are intimately intertwined. One of the basic concepts in āyurveda is that *EVERYTHING* in the world is made up of varying proportions of the Pança Māha Bhutas, or Five Great Elements: Earth, Water, Fire, Air (or Wind, interchangeably), and Ether (or Space). When I initially heard of this, I could wrap my head around four of the elements, but Space? Was that like outer space? What was the difference between Air and Space? Turns out that in āyurveda, when we're talking about Space, we are referring to physical space, as in the space your physical body exists in and occupies right now. If you choose to get up and get yourself a drink of water, you'll move out of your current place and move through new space to find water; simultaneously, you'll leave potential space behind you. In order to have a basic background understanding in āyurveda and its contributions to Elemental-Wellness, let's talk about the elements and consider the qualities (or gunas) of each a bit more.

Space (or Ether) is the most **subtle** of the Five Elements—you can't see it or feel it, you just know it's there, kind of like having faith. Space is **clear**—you can see right through it. Space is **cool**—have you ever noticed that when you go to a higher elevation, like a mountain top, it feels cooler there? Or that when you're feeling hot and crowded, having space around you can help you to feel a bit cooler? Space is **light**—you can measure it by placing boundaries or barriers, but essentially Space is weightless. And Space is *dry*—you don't feel any moisture or humidity in Space.

Air (or Wind) shares some qualities with Space: Air is **subtle, clear, cool, light, and dry.** The biggest difference between these two elements is that Air is the only element that is **mobile.** In āyurveda, Air is the only element that has the quality of movement and is thereby responsible for moving all of the other elements. Because it moves, Air is also **rough**—as Air passes over a surface, like your skin, it can be grating, chafing, or irritating. Finally, Air is considered to be **hard** as opposed to soft. When you think about it, we even have phrases or sayings like "it felt like a harsh wind," and "the wind smacked me in the face." Even though we can't see it, Wind packs a punch!

Fire is **light** and **dry** like Space and Air, but not quite as subtle—Fire is the first element that we can actually see with our eyes. Fire is **hot**—you can definitely appreciate this if you've ever been burned! Fire is **sharp/piercing**—it penetrates or cuts through whatever it contacts, **transforming (digesting)** in the process. Fire is **spreading**—unless it's contained by a barrier of rocks or a fireplace/pit that it can't easily burn through, it permeates and propagates itself. Fire can also be **pungent/ smelly**—you notice how things become more aromatic when you add heat with cooking, or even downright stinky when you burn certain substances. Finally, Fire can be somewhat **oily,** as it **changes** what it burns into a more liquid state.

Water is more substantive than Fire. Water is considered **cool**—unless we're taking a warm bath or a hot shower (which have Fire added to them in the way of heat, by the way), we generally seek naturally occurring water (lakes, rivers, pools) to cool off in hot weather. Water is **fluid**—in its liquid state, it flows. Even in its solid state of ice, water is **lubricating** and can slide over itself and other objects. Water is naturally **smooth**—we're familiar with phrases like lake water being "as smooth as glass"—unless it's perturbed by Air moving over it and causing waves or turbulence. Water is **dull,** as opposed to piercing, sharp, and penetrating. Water is **heavy**—the reason that we can float is because water is heavier and more dense than our physical bodies.

Finally, Earth is the most **gross**, in the sense of being physically tangible and measurable, of all Five Great Elements. Earth is **heavy**—think how rocks and trees are very **heavy, solid,** and **stable.** Unless the Air Element moves the trees or the soil, trees are rooted in the soil and don't appreciably move on their own. The Earth Element is **dull**—as opposed to the piercing qualities of Fire that cuts through things. Earth is **cool**—have you ever dug your feet in the sand at the beach and noticed how cool it can be where the sun isn't warming it? Earth, especially when combined with Water, can be **smooth, oily, sticky,** and **emollient.** Even though we generally think of rocks as being hard, Earth as a Great Element is thought of as being **soft**, as in the texture of clay. And in contrast to the clarity of Space, Earth is **cloudy/opaque.**

Five Great Elements (Panca Mahā Bhutas)

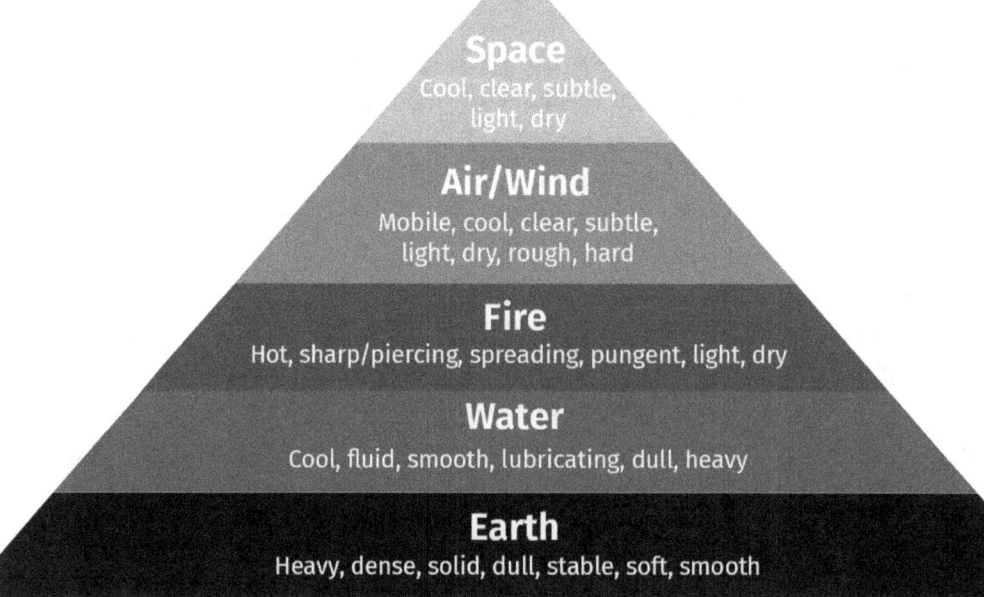

Okay, you say, that's interesting, but what does this have to do with understanding myself and the world around me? Remember that āyurveda views *the whole world and everything in it* as being composed of varying amounts of the Five Great Elements. Recognizing the elements in yourself leads to greater self-awareness and the ability to understand your tendencies. From this vantage point, you can make *choices* that align with your ideal wellness. Invariably, you'll fall off track from time to time. Elemental-Wellness provides tools and insights to recognize ways to self-correct sooner than later, and to course-correct. To make things even simpler, āyurveda breaks things down into just three subtypes, or doshas, of which every living thing is composed. Let's take a look at the doshas.

Doshas

The word *dosha* means "fault" or "that which is vitiated/spoiled." Right out of the gate, āyurveda acknowledges that we are all fallible people who make mistakes and are continual works in progress.

Whew! What a relief! Having been somewhat of a perfectionist for most of my life, I cherish the idea that no one and nothing is perfect, nor is perfection the ultimate goal. You and I can just let go of the idea that we need to meet some unrealistically high standards that don't actually exist.

While it's a commonly accepted truth that you can go further in life by utilizing your strengths than you can by improving your weaknesses, you can still benefit from understanding your weak spots. In fact, you can flourish by recognizing your weaknesses so that they don't trip you up as frequently. It would be akin to knowing that you have one weak ankle and taking steps (no pun intended) to strengthen the supporting muscles while also avoiding falling into a crack or hole in the ground that could cause your weak ankle to twist—a heightened awareness, if you will.

The same is true of other physical, cognitive, and energetic weaknesses. For instance, if you know that you are a slow learner, you can develop strategies to help you learn at your own pace and in your own style. That might look like taking detailed notes as you study a new topic or asking for a mentor to supervise you until you feel more proficient at a task. Likewise, if you know that you tend to get really irritable if you go too long between meals, you can plan ahead or pack yourself a healthy snack if you anticipate a disruption in your routine.

What exactly are these doshas that we speak of? There are three doshas, or constitution types, of which we are all composed. Each of us is made up of varying degrees or percentages of each dosha, and these ratios are said to be determined from the moment of conception—how's that for understanding genetics thousands of years ago without the benefit of microscopes and "modern science"? This is just one of the areas where blending the best of Western and traditional medicines is exciting and makes sense!

DNA (deoxyribonucleic acid, or the stuff that genes are made of) was first discovered in 1869 by Friedrich Miescher, a Swiss chemist, but it wasn't until later in the 20th century that its true role in heredity was better understood. The Human Genome Project, which sequenced the entire genome (all the genetic information of an organism or living being) for Homo sapiens (human beings) was completed only as recently as 2003. So it's mind-boggling that ancient Indians actually had this understanding of how our physical and mental states, even our personalities to a large degree, are inherited from our parents at the moment of conception!

Again, what we inherit in the mix of doshas is neither good nor bad. The goal is *not* to be made of precisely 33.3333 percent of each dosha (unless that is your particular healthiest composition). There is no ideal ratio to be achieved. So again, we are all perfectly perfect, or perfectly imperfect, exactly the way we are. I like the notion that each of us is to be respected as the individual that we are. There is no one-size-fits-all in Elemental-Wellness. You honor your genetic makeup by trying to be your best self, not by following a strict diet, exercise program, or other regimen. Even the word regimen sounds strictly systematic and unwaveringly militaristic! Let's not be rigid when it comes to your health and well-being.

Not surprisingly, the doshas, like everything in āyurveda, are made up of the Five Great Elements. Here I'll highlight each of the doshas.

Vāta

Vāta dosha is made up of primarily the Wind or Air Element and, to a lesser degree, Space. Considering the qualities, or gunas, of these two elements, vāta dosha is *light, clear, subtle, rough, cool, dry, and mobile*. Individuals who are predominantly vāta in their physical makeup tend to be naturally thin, have light bone structure, and are at the extremes of stature—either very tall or very short and bird-like. In Western medicine, they're referred to as ectomorphs. They tend to have fine features and small, dark eyes. They may have thin or dry hair and skin, small or narrow teeth (hypodontia or even anodontia, where they are congenitally missing a complete complement of teeth), and brittle nails. They tend to talk quickly and profusely, and their voice may be quiet and high-pitched, or alternatively it may be very strident and grating.

Vāta dominants tend to be light sleepers who may have difficulty falling asleep or maintaining sleep (insomnia), who are easily awakened from sleep, and who believe they require very little sleep (sometimes six hours or less, despite studies that show that generally adults require about seven to seven-and-a-half hours of quality, restorative sleep). Since this is the only dosha that is mobile, people with a generous amount of vāta tend to move continuously and very quickly, or move in seemingly multiple directions at once. They also think quickly, so they are quick learners, but because their attention can be scattered and intermittent, they tend to be easily distracted and forget just as quickly as they learned. This may look like someone who believes they are multitasking and doing a lot all at once, when actually they are ping-ponging or toggling back and forth between tasks and may not be accomplishing much at all despite the appearance of being "very busy." At the extreme, these may be very bright persons who also live with attention deficit hyperactivity disorder.

What are the advantages to having a healthy dose of vāta? Think of the alphabet: "**A**" is for artistic, "**B**" is for brainstormer, "**C**" is creative, "**D**" is dreamer, and "**E**" is energetic and enthusiastic! In fact, if it wasn't for vāta dosha, nothing would ever get done! Vātas make excellent cheerleaders, collaborators, and social connectors, and also thrive in creative careers in marketing, design, and the arts. Physically, vātas do well in activities that require speed, grace, and expression. This can include dancing, figure skating, and even long-distance running like a gazelle. While vātas tend to get things started, they may get distracted and lack the discipline to see things through. Interesting, right? And yes, there are two other doshas!

Pitta

Pitta dosha is made up of primarily the Fire Element and, to a lesser degree, Water. Combining these qualities, pitta dosha is *hot, sharp, piercing/penetrating, spreading, pungent, fluid, slightly oily, and transformative.* Individuals who are predominantly pitta in their physical makeup tend to be naturally average in body height and weight, and may tend to be slightly muscular or athletic in their build. In Western medicine, pittas are generally considered to be mesomorphs. Their features are average sized, although their complexion may be ruddy or prone to rashes and breakouts, and they may have auburn or strawberry highlights in their hair.

Their most outstanding feature is their eyes—pitta eyes can be piercing, penetrating, and intense, as if they can see right into or through you. Pitta voices tend to be moderate in pace and pitch, and their speech is direct and deliberate, almost punctuated with bullet points. Pitta dominants thrive on around seven-and-a-half hours of sleep, more or less. Their movement is very purposeful—pittas generally prefer the most direct route from point A to point B, as opposed to meandering aimlessly along the scenic route. Pittas are moderate learners and prefer that new learning is presented or broken down into digestible pieces of information, which they tend to retain at an average level. This may look like someone who is very organized and scheduled, and prefers to have a plan instead of just "winging it."

What are the advantages to pitta dosha? When you think "pitta" you can think "**ORG**anized." Pitta dominant people tend to be **Organized**, deliberate, scheduled, and planned. They are very goal-oriented and results driven. Their energy can be **Radiant**—they have a clear vision and can articulate it to others, which gives them a charismatic aura. Along with these abilities, pittas possess a strong digestive system, not just for food, but also for transforming ideas and information. They take concepts from various sources, break down the components, and synthesize information into new applications. This gives them the capacity to be **Great** leaders. And in what exercise do they excel? Just about anything they commit to—pittas are generally athletic and agile so they can enjoy a variety of sports and activities. Due to the strong Fire and Water Elements, pittas may exhibit hypermobile joints and are prone to overuse injuries if they don't strengthen and balance the muscles that support and stabilize joints.

Do any of these things sound familiar? Perhaps. There's one more dosha to check out. Read on!

Kapha

Kapha dosha is made up primarily of the Earth Element and, to a lesser degree, Water. Considering these qualities, kapha dosha is *heavy, dull, cool, oily, smooth, dense/ solid, soft, stable, gross* (meaning tangible/measurable/substantial, *not* repulsive), *and cloudy.* Individuals who are predominantly kapha in their physical makeup tend to have solid body types with dense bone structure and accumulation of muscle and/or fat mass. In Western medicine, they are referred to as endomorphs. Their features are large and rich: large eyes and teeth, luxurious and abundant hair, smooth and supple skin, and strong nails. Perhaps their most notable physical feature is their smile—it is bright, beaming, and beautiful!

Kapha individuals move slowly—no matter how hard you try, you're just not going to rush a true kapha! They will get to their destination, slowly and deliberately, in their own time. Knowing this, they may learn to allow themselves extra time and actually tend to arrive early. Kaphas also tend to be slow learners and may have come to feel badly about this fact. However, once kaphas develop strategies (like making copious, detailed notes) and commit something to learning, they have fantastic memories! Kaphas are not just slow in movement, they are also slow-paced with speech. They may have a lower-pitched voice that is either melodious (think soul singers!) or resonant like a preacher. And as for sleep? You guessed it, kaphas LOVE their sleep—it is long, deep, sound, and restful; at least eight to nine hours is preferred.

What are the advantages of kapha dosha? When you think "kapha," you can think of the kap-acity (that's a little made-up hybrid word combining "kapha" and "capacity") of an elephant! Elephants are great examples of what make kaphas beautiful: they are strong, large, nurturing, loving, loyal, stable, and have great memories. Kapha individuals are the best friends and most loving family members—they're thoughtful and always remember to acknowledge birthdays and other important occasions. They seem to tirelessly give of themselves, perhaps to a fault, and want to patiently take care of others.

For this reason, kaphas make wonderful parents, teachers, and *health care providers*! When it comes to being an employee, they are reliable, dependable, on time and rarely call out sick. They remember and tend to details. Their constitutions are regular and stable, which lends them to regular bowel movements (yes, ancient medicine relied on the quality of one's poop to understand an individual's health and state of relative balance or imbalance!). Regarding exercise, kaphas may have been the kids who didn't pass the timed running test in gym class. Over time, we've learned how skewed and impractical some of these standardized fitness tests can be. It's truly a wake-up call to what we're teaching and testing in our school systems. Again, let's play to our strengths! Kaphas excel at weightlifting and activities that build and require muscle mass and stamina or endurance. While they might not beat you in a sprint, they can hike or walk for miles and miles, and just keep on going.

Having an idea of your constitution can help you identify your strengths so that you can apply them to your benefit and to the benefit of those around you. You can proactively take care of yourself to enjoy your optimum Elemental-Wellness and ideal well-being.

It's common in today's world to see signs of imbalances. As you reflect on the following self-quiz, if you're uncertain about which choice best describes you, consider what your answer might have been for your younger self between the ages of childhood through your young adult years. Alternatively, you may identify with two or three of the choices fairly equally. When that occurs, go ahead and check both/all three. This is not intended to be an exhaustive list. It is an invitation to greater self-awareness. Enjoy!

Dosha Self-Quiz

Select the statement or statements that best describe you.

1. My physical frame is best described as:
   a) Slight and very tall or diminutive
   b) Average height
   c) Large-framed with dense bones

2. When it comes to weight:
   a) It's difficult for me to put on muscle or gain weight.
   b) I've always hovered around "normal" weight.
   c) I can add muscle or fat easily.

3. My features are generally:
   a) Fine: thin nose/lips/face, slender teeth/spaces between teeth, small eyes
   b) Average in size, and eyes especially bright/penetrating
   c) Large and round: full lips, large eyes and teeth, and a broad smile

4. My skin is:
   a) Dry, flaky, scaly, or wrinkled
   b) Oily, ruddy, or freckled complexion and prone to breakouts, rashes, or blemishes
   c) Smooth, soft, and moist

5. My speech tends to be:
   a) Quick and abundant! And my voice tends to be either very soft or somewhat rough/grating in nature.
   b) Moderate in pitch, speed, and tone. I can speak eloquently and to-the-point.
   c) Slow and low-pitched. I may speak or sing melodiously.

6. I walk:
   a) Quickly and in constant motion, and I may tend to get side-tracked.
   b) Moderately paced and I usually have a distinct path in mind to get to my destination.
   c) Slowly and I can't be rushed, so I may allow extra time in order to arrive early.

7. I learn new concepts:
   a) Quickly, but I may also forget quickly, so I need repetition or other reminders to retain new information.

b) Fairly readily, and retain an average amount as well.

c) More slowly than others. I feel like I have to work harder at learning new things, but once I commit information to memory, I've got it! And I'll remember birthdays and other events that are important to the people in my life.

8. Typically I sleep:
   a) Six hours or less—who needs sleep? Besides, I often have trouble falling or staying asleep and I'm prone to insomnia.
   b) Between seven and seven-and-a-half hours is my sweet spot.
   c) Eight hours or more—the longer and deeper and more luxurious, the better!

9. Regarding appetite:
   a) I prefer to graze or eat multiple smaller meals.
   b) I get hangry if I miss a meal!
   c) I feel fine if I miss a meal or fast intermittently.

10. I tend toward:
    a) Fear, restlessness, and anxiety
    b) Impatience, overwhelm, and obsession with things being done the way I like them to be done
    c) Depression

11. I'm best described as being:
    a) Creative, intuitive, and introspective
    b) Competitive, organized, and efficient
    c) Loyal, dependable, and loving

12. My digestion and elimination:
    a) Tend to be sensitive—I'm prone to constipation, gas, and bloating
    b) Can process just about anything, although I sometimes develop loose stools/diarrhea or acid indigestion
    c) Produce one solid stool regularly each morning

13. When it comes to exercise, I prefer:
    a) Dance or fluid movement sports like skating or tai chi
    b) I'm a natural athlete—I can pick up/play just about any sport, and I tend to be competitive with others or myself.
    c) I'll never set a speed record for running the mile, but I'm strong and have the endurance to walk or hike for miles.

14. In my work life:
    a) I'm a team player, but if I'm unhappy, I'll move on to another position in a heartbeat.
    b) I'm very focused, driven, and goal-oriented. I have a vision and I'm frequently in leadership positions.
    c) I'm the first one to arrive, and I don't leave until the job is done. I have worked in the same position/organization for years.

15. My ideal vacation:
    a) Is full of possibilities and activities—I'm open to trying it all!
    b) Has a specific itinerary—I've researched my options and planned ahead.
    c) Has plenty of downtime to rest and relax, maybe lounging around the resort pool with a good book or trying out some local foods.

16. Regarding relationships:
    a) I have many friends and I love to get different friend groups together for parties and reunions. On the flip side, my feelings also get hurt easily.
    b) I don't have much interest in spending time with people who don't share similar interests and values. I'm discerning with whom I surround myself.
    c) I'm always there for friends and family. I'm loyal, loving, and generous, sometimes to a fault.

17. Describing my strengths:
    a) I'm artistic, creative, and energetic—I get things started!
    b) I'm organized and articulate. I can process information and distill it down into understandable nuggets. I'm driven and goal-oriented.
    c) I'm solid and dependable. There's no hidden agenda. You can rely on me—I've got your back!

Add up your responses. If you identified mostly with "A" tendencies, your dominant dosha is likely vāta. If you selected mostly "B" responses, you probably have a strong pitta constitution. And if you chose mostly "C" answers, your makeup is primarily kapha in quality. If you identified strongly with two of the three doshas, you may be a strong blend of both. Others are fairly tri-doshic, identifying fairly equally with all three traits. Remember, everyone is made up of all three doshas, just in differing amounts. There is no right or wrong; there is no perfect or ideal ratio. *The goal is awareness of your true self.*

> The goal is awareness of your true self.

Knowing your tendencies can help you to be mindful of your pitfalls and shortcomings, so that you can identify them early in order to course-correct more easily. In āyurveda and Elemental-Wellness, we view these snafus as imbalances. In the next section, we'll explore these imbalances as they manifest in your physical and mental health, and consider some strategies that can be employed to regain your balance and well-being, to experience *Bliss, Not Burnout.*

■ ■ ■

How Do Āyurveda and Elemental-Wellness Address Physical and Mental Health?

While it is possible to be imbalanced by having too little of an element or dosha, it's more common that imbalances arise from having *too much* of a good thing. Understanding your personal constitution or makeup through the lens of āyurveda may give you a clue as to where you're likely to become imbalanced.

For example, let's say in the preceding Dosha Self-Quiz, you scored a predominance of pitta qualities. In this section, you will understand how an excess of your pitta qualities might make you more prone to impatience, judgment, frustration, overheating, and feeling "hangry" (hungry and angry). Regardless of your predominant dosha or doshas, you can be mindful that *everyone* is susceptible to *any* imbalance. To continue with the pitta dominant model, if you are mainly pitta in your makeup, you can still experience a vāta or kapha imbalance. In this section, we'll explore how this can be possible and what it looks like.

Since each of us is composed of all five elements and therefore all three doshas, it's helpful to understand each of the imbalances so you can recognize them when they creep up on you, as well as when you see them in others. Health care providers are trained to examine others, in particular to look for what is *wrong* with them, and then to use modern science and Western medicine to "fix" people.

The invitation here is to put down your virtual binoculars (you know, those things you use to scrutinize others, possibly pass judgment, and avoid looking at yourself). Instead, I invite you to pick up your hand mirror and give yourself the gift of self-reflection and introspection so that you can be more self-aware, take better self-care, and exercise greater self-compassion. The by-product is that you will be a better health care provider, team member, friend, family member, and citizen in the community. And it absolutely *must* start with *you.*

Consider again the image of kapha as an elephant.

Elephants symbolize strength, power, wisdom, intelligence, and loyalty. When kaphas have an excess of *heavy, solid, and stable* in their physicality, it can look like being overweight. Occasionally it can be excess muscle mass, as in extreme body building where muscles are overly bulky. More commonly it's seen as excess fat accumulation and a sedentary lifestyle. Mentally, excess *dull, muddy, and cloudy* can manifest as depression, withdrawal, and lack of motivation.

Kapha dominants may have a tendency to be too *soft and sticky*, and can easily become overly attached to people, places, and things. Kaphas may stay in a relationship that is unhealthy or energetically draining long after it's time to move on, and kaphas can be overly attached to relationships—stifling or clinging, identifying more as a couple than as an individual, or being either a "helicopter" parent or a "hovering" adult child of an aging parent. They may overly identify with their place of employment or their home. Changing jobs or moving from their home is extremely emotionally disruptive for kaphas—so painful, in fact, that they may stay in a position for decades even though they feel unhappy and unfulfilled. Kaphas are prone to getting bogged down by the strain and drain of being all things to all people all the time.

> Like increases like; opposites balance.

What is the antidote? A basic principle in āyurveda is that *like increases like; opposites balance*. The two easiest ways to balance are **diet** (by diet we really refer to nutrition, as in what you consume, not a particular type of "brand name" diet) and **activity**. Here's where we draw on the elements again! What are signs of excess kapha? Too much *heavy, sticky, and dull* can show up as lethargy, depression, excessive weight gain and, digestively, the sensation of "brick belly." If a kapha imbalance derives from excessive *dull, muddy, and cloudy*, then the opposites would be increased *bright, sharp, and clear*—essentially using these qualities of Fire, Air, and Space to burn off and dry up excess Earth and Water.

When it comes to food choices and feeling sad or depressed, your first inclination might be to reach for comfort foods that are rich and heavy, like a dense macaroni and cheese followed by a cold bowl of creamy ice cream! Even if you seem to enjoy it in the moment, you know you'll feel worse than ever afterward, and potentially feel heavy, guilty, or ashamed about your choice.

Instead, you'll want to choose the opposite elements of Air and Space: *light, clear, subtle, rough, cool, dry, and mobile*, with a little bit of Fire (spice!). That looks like crisp and fresh fruit, raw or lightly steamed vegetables, dry rice/grains (like saffron-infused basmati rice as opposed to pork fried rice), and lean proteins like legumes or fish/poultry. You can sprinkle in a bit of cayenne (or alternatively citrus) to dry out the sludge and boost your digestion. Fresh, local, and organic are always the best choices. And while it might feel difficult to peel yourself off the couch or even get out of bed and get dressed, you'll benefit from activities that are also *light and mobile*—in other words, uplifting! This could be a Vinyasa-style yoga class, zumba, or another group class (ideally here the teacher is an uplifting and motivational cheerleader, and the other participants provide community), a brisk walk outdoors, or some other refreshing exercise.

The kapha counterbalancing yoga class in Chapter 8 is a sequence for lifting up a kapha overload imbalance. Like any mindful practice, you care for yourself best by being self-aware, modifying the suggested postures and techniques to suit your current abilities. With Elemental-Wellness tools, you know your physical and mental states better than anyone else, and you are uniquely suited to make choices that prevent injury and support your well-being.

■ ■ ■

When you think of pitta dosha, you can envision a lion!

Lions symbolize courage, wisdom, justice, and ferocity. An overabundance of Fire—*hot, sharp, spreading*—can present as anger, frustration, impatience, and irritation. The goal-oriented drive to excel and compete can manifest as harshly overbearing demands. An angry pitta might become so frustrated and impatient that they just steamroll over anyone and anything that gets in their way. After all, no one else can seem to do things the right way—their way!

They may feel that they're the only one who can get things done, and sometimes they just have to seize control, cut through the nonsense, and do it themselves. They are prone to road rage, speaking before thinking and then regretting it later, and being sharply critical of themselves and others. They may be prone to high blood pressure, ulcers, acne, and rashes—all signs of excess Pitta Fire. In extremes, pitta imbalances can be associated with the need to be organized and in charge, as in obsessive compulsive disorders.

Katia talks about the challenges she faces working for decades as a registered nurse:

"Working in health care has made me more stressed. I work so hard to keep my patients well. If a patient is demanding or critical, I can be short with them at times. I'm happy with my personal values and effort, but sometimes I get so frustrated with both the patients and my coworkers! When I'm tired or stressed about work, I tend to be less social outside of work as well."

So what's a lion to do? *Like increases like; opposites balance.* This is not the time to reach for more coffee/caffeine or alcohol—both are heating beverages. It's also not the time to eat extra spicy foods. To tame the Fire-y lion, there needs to be more of the opposites—Earth on one end of the continuum and Space on the other. In other words, foods that are *solid, stable, and cool, as well as light, clear, and dry.* Examples would be clear broth or lightly sautéed vegetables with minimal seasoning, moderate grains like quinoa that are nurturing without being heavy, and regular meals as opposed to skipping a meal or having one large meal and not much else.

Regarding activities when experiencing pitta imbalance, you should *not* go out for a sweaty run in the heat of the day over your lunch break, but consider a brisk walk in the shade or a few minutes of meditation instead. You need to cool down—literally take off a layer of clothing if you're feeling overheated and turn down the heat or get into some air conditioning or a breeze if possible. You shouldn't take a hot yoga or vigorous aerobics class after work—that will only keep your fire stoked! Instead, stopping at a park on the way home to take a walk, grounding yourself in nature and looking up into a clear sky, feeling the space all around you, will be much more restorative (and your family and pets will appreciate you more when you get home!).

Like increases like; opposites balance.

The Pitta Pacifying yoga class that you will find in Chapter 8 is a sequence for soothing a pitta overload imbalance. Like any mindful practice, you care for yourself best by being self-aware, modifying the suggested postures and techniques to suit your current abilities. With Elemental-Wellness tools, you know your physical and mental states better than anyone else, and you are uniquely suited to make choices that prevent injury and support your well-being.

■ ■ ■

What about an excess of vāta dosha? Regardless of your predominant dosha, vāta overload is the most common imbalance in our modern western society. And why is that? Because we are living in an era when information doubles roughly every 12 minutes, as opposed to doubling every century just a handful of decades ago. We are constantly bombarded with messages: advertising, apps, notifications, emails, social media, sights and sounds—it's a recipe for sensory overload! When there is too much vāta dosha, there is an excess of Air and Space, and generally an excess of sound and movement. Picture in your mind's eye a squirrel!

Squirrels are symbols of spirit, playfulness, connection, gratitude, and resourcefulness. Squirrels scurry from one place to another, often erratically. Have you ever watched a squirrel try to cross the street, or have you tried to avoid running one over with your car? It's as if they're scurrying frenetically to hide their nuts, then forgot where they put them and seemingly what was the point of their activity in the first place. And they chitter loudly!

An overabundance of Air and Space—*light, clear, subtle, rough, cool, dry, and mobile*—looks like too much movement, hyperactivity, lack of focus, or distractibility. ADD and ADHD can be viewed as extreme vāta imbalances. All of this is not to say that everyone can be cured simply by balancing their doshas. If you are struggling with a hormonal imbalance or any medical disorder, please seek medical attention. If a particular medication is beneficial, you should not self-adjust your dosage or discontinue medication without the advice and assistance of your medical provider.

The Vāta Validating yoga class coming up in Chapter 8 is a sequence for grounding a vāta overload imbalance. Like any mindful practice, you care for yourself best by being self-aware, modifying the suggested postures and techniques to suit your current abilities. With Elemental-Wellness tools, you know your physical and mental states better than anyone else, and you are uniquely suited to make choices that prevent injury and support your well-being.

■ ■ ■

To be clear, none of this information is intended solely to diagnose or treat any disorder or disease! This is not a substitute for individualized medical care, diagnosis, or treatment. **This tradition *is* intended to expand and complement your current vision of your wellness and the world you live in.** By considering life through the lens of the Elements, āyurveda and Elemental-Wellness expand your perspective and mindstate so that you can observe yourself and the world more objectively.

Generally speaking, the physical wellness goals are:

- To keep your joints mobile and lubricated
- To keep your muscles strong and supple through a balance of strengthening and stretching
- To maintain cardiovascular fitness and endurance
- To align your physical body so that you observe healthy ergonomics as much as possible

That last one can be quite the challenge in health care, as you adapt to serving your patients! As a practicing dentist, I've found myself in some interesting postures—a la a Cirque du Soleil contortionist—in order to visualize the dark depths of my patients' oral cavities. There's always a patient who "can't tip back" because they can't breathe, requiring me to virtually stand on my head to perform microsurgery.

There may be various reasons why patients say they can't tip back. Some may have neck or back issues, including kyphosis and osteoporosis, that limit their cervical range of motion. Victims of abuse and trauma, especially victims of oral sexual abuse, are likely to feel especially vulnerable being tipped back with their mouth wide open. These individuals may share their experience with me as their health care provider, or they may not feel able to tell me their history, and I am only left to wonder and compassionately help them to help themselves (more on this in the section on breathing).

Others may have physical breathing restrictions from COPD, emphysema, and connective tissue/degenerative disorders. Patients may also feel like they have postnasal drip, which interestingly manifests mainly when they recline. Whenever I hear this, my radar perks up to screen for signs of impaired breathing, snoring, and apnea: Is there an enlarged or elongated uvula, large or cryptic tonsils, or simply excess mucosal tissue in the back of the throat? Could there be an oversized tongue that exhibits either scalloping on the lateral borders from friction against the teeth, or ankyloglossia ("tongue tie") that keeps the tongue tethered to the floor of the mouth and back of the throat instead of being able to extend forward and out of the airway? (Again, more on this in the chapter on breathing.)

■ ■ ■

"A" is for Attitude

Attitude is actually a choice, in the same way that perspective is a choice. The saying goes that everyone is entitled to their first *reaction* to their feelings. What you choose to do next is your opportunity to self-regulate and choose an appropriate *response*. There's a reason that we use the expression "knee-jerk *reaction*." When a stimulus is sent only to the spinal cord, you experience a quick *reaction*. When your hand contacts a hot frying pan, you don't have to think about it, you automatically remove your hand from the hot stimulus. Then, when the pain signal is sent to your brain to interpret it, you choose how to *respond*—turn down the heat on the frying pan, run cool water over your burned hand (or not, if you assess that it isn't that bad).

Similarly, when an emotional or intellectual stimulus is uncomfortable, your first feeling is your *reaction*. It's easy to stay stuck here in your reptilian brain, the amygdala, where you're still not using your whole brain with your reasoning and problem-solving skills. With a bit of perspective, you get to choose your *response*. Here's what that looks like in real time:

On a Friday morning at the end of a long week, I had an extra hour to get to work before my first patient. Enjoying a few extra minutes of unrushed time, I intentionally decided to take the leisurely route to the office, meandering past some farms and scenic riverways. At precisely 8:02, my cell phone rang, and caller ID alerted me that it was my office calling me. I picked up the call.

"Hello, Dawn," I said. "You're not calling to wish me a good morning, are you?"

Dawn replied, "I wish I was!"

Apparently, the hygienist who was due in for a working interview (who had visited the office previously and with whom I had spoken at length over the phone) had not arrived for her 8:00 a.m. patient. When Dawn shared this wonderful news, along with the fact that the hygienist also let Dawn's phone call go to her voicemail, I let out a big sigh and chuckled. "Of course she's not there."

The "old" me might have reacted. The previous me might have gotten angry and flustered and reactive. The "new" me, the one that believes in Bliss, Not Burnout, *took a moment to breathe first, and to respond second. The new me didn't get stuck in the problem; the new me went into solution-focus. I had been looking forward to a lighter schedule myself so I could catch up on some administrative and paperwork duties, so I knew I had flexibility in my schedule. We could scramble and try to find a hygienist to fill in on short notice, or we could band together and combine my schedule with the hygienist's schedule.*

Collaborating with my team, we were able to sort out the day so that we only had to reappoint one patient while delivering optimal care to the other patients. I was tired and needed to find another time for my administrative duties, but it still felt less stressful to focus on solutions *rather than* problems.

Points to Ponder

- What has been your default approach to difficult situations in the past?
- How might pausing to respond with solutions to challenges be less stressful than reacting to problems going forward?

■ ■ ■

"A" is for Appreciation

It's been said that it can take 10 to 20 positive or complimentary statements to balance out just one negative or derogatory remark. Even when we don't perceive a comment as being negative, the recipient may take offense or interpret feedback as a personal criticism. As a boss and leader, I remind myself to thank and praise my team both publicly

Identify the **specific behavior**, the **need that was met,** and the **positive feeling** you experienced as a result.

(in front of patients or other team members) and privately (one-on-one) throughout the day with a simple "Thank you for all your hard work today."

I thought that was enough, and then I learned that I could up my game by being more specific. Gratitude and **Appreciation** are important ingredients in any relationship, and to really make them count, it's best to get more specific: identify the **specific behavior**, the **need that was met,** and the **positive feeling** you experienced as a result. For example, rather than just thanking my team for pitching in to care for all of our patients when the hygienist no-showed on us:

*I thanked Dawn for calling me so we could come up with a solution together (**specific behavior**). I thanked her for rescheduling the one patient we could not accommodate, letting her know that I **needed her support** so that the schedule was doable, and that there was structure and a system in place so we could be successful in delivering optimal care. I **felt more grounded** and supported.*

*As for my assistants, I thanked them for swiftly setting up rooms, reviewing medical histories, exposing radiographs and wellness scans, and wrapping up one patient appointment so I could move on to the next (**specific behavior**). Again, I **needed their help** to accomplish necessary tasks. I appreciated that they took extra time to use the intraoral camera to review areas of concern with patients, because I **felt supported** and capable of achieving our goals. I **needed teamwork and collaboration**, and I appreciated that everyone pitched in together. Instead of feeling stressed and harried, I **felt successful** and enjoyed all of our patients.* Bliss, Not Burnout.

Points to Ponder

- How and how often do you currently demonstrate appreciation for your coworkers, family, and friends?
- In order to have an even greater impact, how can you be even more specific with your appreciations in the future?

5

"B" IS FOR BREATH AND BREATHING

Exhale . . . yes, right now! Exhale completely, then allow your breath to naturally enter back into your body. Exhale again, squeezing all the stale air out of your lungs. Allow your "gills" to fill naturally without effort. Now exhale one more time with a little sigh.

How do you feel? Is there any sense of release? Have any muscles in your head, neck, or shoulders relaxed just a bit? How are your thoughts? Is there heightened present-moment awareness? Even if only one micron of your being has ticked a smidgeon (that is a scientific term of measurement, of course) toward the direction of peace and presence, you are experiencing the power of breath control, which is a beautiful skill.

If you've noticed no release or even experienced increased agitation, that is noteworthy and valuable feedback as well. Over-efforting can lead to lightheadedness, achiness, irritability, and frustration. Now that you've been introduced to the elements and the doshas, you may recognize over-effort and overexertion as excess Fire or pitta. It's not necessarily a good or bad thing, it's more the question of "How does that work for you?" If you find yourself feeling pitta imbalance in this breath exercise, perhaps try softening a bit, not squeezing as strongly on the exhale, and then *permitting* the new air to enter your airway as opposed to actively inhaling. Let yourself try this again, with a little more softness or even dullness in your gaze. Consider closing your eyes or lowering your eyelids so that you look gently toward the ground.

How did that go? Did you notice any difference? If you did, then you learned a new adjustment that may be helpful. If you didn't notice a difference, that's okay, too! Just keep practicing. It may be that you need to step away from the exercise and try again at another time. It's possible that you're still cultivating self-awareness and that these subtle shifts are not so noticeable to you at this moment. And it could also be that you're simply new to this type of experience, and with repetition over time you may realize other outcomes. Bottom line: it's all good. There's no wrong here, there's just your experience. There's no success versus failure, there's only your lived perception.

What if this little exercise caused you to feel sleepy or logy, and you'd rather feel more alert so you can continue to read this book (or do any other activity)? While this outcome is less likely to occur, perhaps you were already feeling pretty relaxed and now you feel sedated. This is a good self-observation! You can take your sense of presence and grounding and bring them into movement or action. Stand up! Move your arms, shake your hands and feet, walk around a little. Now when you sit down to read or focus on a task, you can enjoy renewed centering.

What do we call this breathing technique? This is an example of "mindful breathing." It is intended to be a simple technique that you can employ anytime, anywhere, in less than a minute. No one else needs to know you're doing it, unless you share it with them. It is absolutely free, requires no special clothing or equipment, and is available to everyone. This is just the beginning of the power of breath.

Pranayama

In yoga, the word prana means "life force" and yama means "restraint," so together the word pranayama refers to control (restraint) of life force energy via the breath. When you think about it, most of us take breathing for granted, as it happens automatically about 20,000 to 25,000 times per day, or about 8,000,000 times each year, without us ever giving it a conscious thought. Medically speaking, breathing is driven by the autonomic nervous system, the same part of your nervous system that controls other unconscious bodily processes, including contraction of your heart, peristaltic movements of your intestines, and other vital organ functions, like when your pancreas secretes insulin and when your liver converts stored energy into glucose that is released for cellular use. These vital activities happen whether we're awake or asleep.

Unlike controlling your liver function, however, your breath is actually something you can also control consciously. Hence, pranayama is *breath control*. When you practice conscious and mindful breathing, you are practicing a form of mindfulness meditation. When your attention is on your breath—the feel of it, the sound of it, the shape and size of it and its rhythm—you are practicing single-minded focus. Depending on what your particular needs are at any given moment, you can use your breath to sharpen your focus or to soften your intensity. You can use your breath to energize your body and mind, or to ground yourself. You can use the breath to warm up or to cool down. Let's consider some different practices.

Centering and Performance-Enhancing Breath: Nasal Breathing and Five-Second Breath

In his book *Breath: The New Science of a Lost Art*, scientific journalist James Nestor elucidates the importance of both inhaling and exhaling for five seconds each, creating a slow, rhythmic cycle that is efficient and grounding. He cites historical chants, songs, and mantras that are considered to be soothing. The main thing they all have in common is that they correspond to a five-second inhalation and exhalation.

Like most breathing exercises, this can be practiced while standing, sitting, or lying down. It can be helpful to have an elongated, aligned torso, to the best of your ability. If you're standing, plant your feet firmly, either hip- or shoulder-width apart, standing tall and straight. If you're seated in a chair, it's best to come out to the edge of the chair so that you're almost perching at the edge, with your feet again planted firmly on the floor. If you're seated on the floor, it can be helpful to have your hips elevated on a block or cushion.

To practice the five-second breath, first exhale completely, giving a little extra squeeze at the end of your regular exhalation. This eliminates more stale/stagnant air from your lungs, thus creating space for more complete inhalation. Then, with your next natural inspiration, breathe in slowly to the count of five seconds. Pause at the top of your inhalation and reverse the flow in a five-second exhalation. Pause again at the bottom of your breath before beginning your next round of five-second inhalation-pause-exhalation-pause, forming a smooth, fluid rhythm. If it feels like it's too long, like you're not able to breathe in and out for that long, just slow things down as much as possible, easing your way into a five-second breath.

Just about everyone can hold their breath for five seconds, so rationally you can inhale for that long and exhale in the same way. If it helps, you can imagine your lungs to be a balloon that can inflate slowly and smoothly, and that you can control the release of air so that the balloon doesn't make an obscene noise and sputter all around the room as air releases too quickly! The simple act of focusing on the breath in this manner is calming and centering, contributing to improved focus and function.

Slowing down your breath can actually make you more effective and efficient both mentally and physically! With increased focus, you're able to accomplish tasks more accurately and easily the first time, leaving fewer errors and corrections to make. Conditioning your physical body to breathe through the nose for five-second breaths improves physical and athletic performance for endurance activities. Sure, there are times when short bursts of breath or more rapid breathing can be helpful or more practical, but the more you practice five-second breathing, the more benefits you'll discover.

Breathing to Heighten Presence and Self-Awareness: Dirgha (Three-Part Complete Breath)

The most basic yogic breath practice is called dirgha, or three-part complete yogic breath. The objectives of the three-part breath are to become more embodied and to increase your self-awareness in the present moment. Complete breathing also promotes healthy posture and massages the vital organs of digestion and elimination, providing greater lung capacity and improved assimilation and detoxification.

With the demands of everyday life and the additional challenges of caring for others as a health care provider, it's easy to become disembodied, or literally detached from your own awareness and experiences. The beauty of this dirgha basic building block is that it is so versatile and can be practiced in any position, in any location, at any time. You can literally practice while standing in line at the grocery store in order to remain patient and relaxed, or while performing microsurgery in order to stay calm, clear, and focused!

If you're unfamiliar with this technique, and even if you are a seasoned veteran to this breath, it can be helpful to practice with the eyes of a beginner by lying on your back. First, make yourself comfortable on a firm surface. A yoga mat on the floor is perfect for this, and you can also practice in bed. However, an overly fluffy sofa might suck you in and not support you as well. While lying down, make sure there is no pain in your lower back, spine, or neck area. If there is lower back pain, you can bring your feet shoulder-width or wider, bend your knees so that your feet are flat on the floor (or bed), and allow your knees to touch together. This usually relieves tension from commonly overstretched muscles in the lower back.

Now bring both hands to your belly, palms facing down, and wrap your thumbs around your waist toward your back (think of standing with your hands on your hips/waist, except you're lying down horizontally). Exhale completely as in the five-second breath, then slowly inhale low into your abdomen (you can certainly use the five-second breath technique here as well!), feeling your belly rise in front of you and simultaneously noticing your waist expanding to both sides. Perhaps you can feel your lower back expanding toward the floor beneath you, so that your entire belly breath is expanding your lower abdomen. Breathe in and out for a few cycles in this way.

Now slide your hands up to your ribs, so that your fingers are splayed over the front of your ribcage and the thumbs wrap around toward your back. With the next inhalation, bring your attention to your mid-torso, expanding the ribs in all directions. Notice the ribs elevating not just your front body, but also expanding to either side and pressing your back firmly against the ground. Continuing to breathe in this way for a few breath cycles, you can appreciate how the breath is not something that just happens in the front of your body, but it involves your whole midsection in all dimensions.

Finally, slide the hands up toward your chest so that your palms cover your chest/pectoral muscles, your fingertips touch your clavicles or collar bones, and your thumbs tuck into your armpits. Now bring your attention to filling the upper lobes of the lungs, noticing the subtle lift of your hands as you inhale, and perhaps also feeling your thumbs get a gentle squeeze as your chest inflates, your vastus lateralis muscles expand, and your mid- and upper-back muscles engage the floor. Take a few breaths here, just noticing, witnessing, paying attention, breathing mindfully. Next, leave one hand on the chest and slide the other back toward your belly.

Begin to combine all three aspects of the complete breath, inhaling and expanding first the lower abdomen, the ribs, and then the upper torso and chest. Exhale the opposite way, allowing first the chest to recede, then the ribs to relax, and finally the belly to contract toward the spine. Again, take several breath cycles in this way. Try not to exert too much effort or try too hard—allow the breath to be full and complete and also organic and natural.

When you feel that this breath is complete for you, let go of the control and allow whatever breathing flows naturally to happen. Keep your focus inward, and notice what's shifted for you: Are you feeling more grounded? More spacious? More focused? Perhaps bored or agitated? Anything is possible! And whatever comes up can be witnessed without judgment.

Calming Breath:
Taking Nasal Breathing and Dirgha to a Different Level

What happens when you find yourself agitated, impatient, annoyed, angry, overwhelmed, or frustrated? Or perhaps you're feeling anxious, nervous, scared, insecure, or unsure? It's normal for all of us to cycle through these emotions.

Having tools of awareness and also having some "tools in your emotional toolbelt" can be helpful to manage these feelings. If you're feeling stressed at work, it isn't healthy or helpful to spiral out of control and have a temper tantrum (sadly, we've likely all witnessed this, even from the person who's supposed to be the leader in charge!). Likewise, if you have an upcoming presentation, whether it's a lecture or a case presentation, or you've got difficult news to share with a patient and their loved ones, it can be helpful to compose yourself before you deliver your message. Go ahead and give yourself a little breathing break. If you need to go to the restroom to have a couple of minutes to yourself, hopefully no one will follow you there! And if anyone does notice you breathing, who cares? You might inspire them to do the same.

Building on the combination of nasal and three-part dirgha breathing, you can help to ground yourself by lengthening the exhalation. For instance, let's say you've just inspired smoothly through your nose to a five-second count. (If it's comfortable, you can be more meditative or introspective by either closing your eyes or softening and lowering your gaze.) Upon expiration, slow down the release of breath through your nose so that it takes a bit longer, maybe six or seven seconds, for you to exhale completely. Allow the breath to follow the releasing pattern of the upper lobes (collar bones, back of the heart), chest (ribs—front, back, and sides), and belly (squeezing the stale air from the lower lobes, pressing your belly button toward the direction of your spine).

With the next breath sequence, again inhale for five seconds, and this time lengthen your exhalation to eight seconds with the same pattern. You can continue to breathe in for five seconds and gradually lengthen your outbreaths by an additional second until you've reached a one-to-two ratio (5 seconds inhalation: 10 seconds exhalation) or even longer if that's within your comfort and ability and you find it to be calming and relaxing. As with any exercise, if you feel physically or mentally uncomfortable, you can stop at any time and/or modify. And like other exercises, you can increase your capacity and endurance with practice over time.

Energizing Breath
(Variation of "Pulling Prana")

So far we've talked about how synchronizing the breath to five seconds promotes optimal oxygenation and centering, how three-part complete breathing enhances self-awareness and centering, and how lengthening your exhalations can relieve stress, tension, and worry. There are other times when your energy can be less than desired, when you have that feeling of wanting to lie on the couch or go back to bed versus facing responsibilities and addressing the day's agenda. Perhaps you could actually use some more sleep, but you're facing yet another 12-hour shift and sleep is a distant dream. The good news is that, in addition to using your breath to calm and center yourself, you can also use your breath to elevate your energy!

One of my favorite energizing breaths is a variation of "pulling prana"—literally drawing in life-force energy. Like many breathing exercises, with a little creativity this can be practiced while lying down, sitting, or standing. The easiest way to understand this technique is to start from standing. (See the Kapha Counter-Balance section in Chapter 8.)

Remember to use nasal breathing, and step one foot about a leg's length distance from the other foot, coming into goddess pose (deviasana), or horse stance. Bend your elbows and bring your arms to shoulder level at your sides like "goal posts." Inhale your elbows back just an inch, and then exhale the elbows toward each other in front of your chest and face. They don't need to touch, it's just a direction you're moving in. With the next inhalation, reach both arms up overhead. As you begin to exhale, bend your elbows and pull them down by your side ribs, simultaneously making fists by your shoulders. With the next breath, extend both arms out in front of you at the horizon, palms facing down. As you exhale, draw your elbows by your sides and pull energy into your hands as you make them into fists facing your armpits. Repeat this sequence using the five-second breath, visualizing pulling energy from your surroundings and drawing it into your physical and mental body with each breath cycle.

As you become familiar with the series, feel free to increase the pace of your breath—here is when it's okay to abandon the five-second breath! Swift inhalations and sharp exhalations are enlivening. If you're standing in goddess or horse stance and want to take it up a notch, you can alternately lift one knee on the inhalation and set that foot down on the exhalation at the same time that you're breathing in sync with the arm sequence. I affectionately call this the "Funky Monkey"! It's a fun favorite that I've shared while teaching yoga to students with Down syndrome. Alternatively, it is not the best choice for individuals who struggle with schizophrenia, mania, oppositional defiant disorder, or nervous anxiety, as it has the potential to exacerbate or aggravate these conditions. If this exercise causes you to feel short of breath, dizzy, or disoriented, you have overdone it. You can slow things down by returning to basic belly breathing, allowing your belly to expand with the inbreath like a baby and then just naturally receding on the outbreath without any significant effort.

Points to Ponder

- How often do you notice your breathing? Are you able to breathe through your nose? While it's normal to alternately breathe more through one nostril than the other throughout the day, an inability to breathe through your nose with your lips sealed warrants a medical consultation.
- How might you use your breath and some of the breathing techniques in this chapter to support your self-care and well-being?
- What reminders or habits can you link to checking in with your breath in order to experience greater *Bliss, Not Burnout*? (For instance, maybe you could set a reminder or alarm on your phone or computer every hour or a few times throughout the day. Could you link a breathing check-in to every time you use the restroom, or walk into a room? Get creative here!)

6

"C" IS FOR CONNECTIONS, CAREGIVING, AND COMMUNICATION

Connections Between Modern Science and Collective Wisdom

Āyurveda dates back thousands of years, arguably 4,000 to 5,000 years, according to many sources. The fact that these rishis, or sages, understood so much about human anatomy, physiology, and psychology without the aid of modern scientific instruments and research is astounding! When you think about it, they were describing what happens on cellular and molecular levels without using a microscope to visualize microbes and cell structure.

While not everything in traditional medicines would hold up to today's standards, there are some striking comparative similarities. For example, we generally frown upon the idea of using blood-sucking leeches as a form of medical therapy, but we *do* cleanse blood through dialysis and also transfuse blood from one human to another, so we're really not that far astray from the ancients. And how in the world could they know so much about digestive processes, for example, without microscopes, including endoscopy and colonoscopy?

The fact is, much of an āyurvedic evaluation focuses on the quality of one's stool (feces) to determine relative balances and imbalances. In short, there's a lot of "talking shit." But that shouldn't be off-putting or come as a surprise. Consider veterinary medicine for a moment. When you take your canine to the vet, whether for a sick or well visit, what are the most common intake questions? They want to know about your dog's thirst and appetite. What does their diet consist of? How is their elimination? Frequency of urination? Quantity and quality of bowel movements? What is your canine's activity like? So basically, there is a great emphasis on diet, digestion, and exercise.

In pediatric medicine, particularly with newborn babies, the inquiry is much the same. How is your child's thirst and appetite? What and when are they eating and drinking? How often are they moving their bowels and what is the color and consistency? Also, what is their activity? How are they sleeping? How is their skin tone, color, texture, and temperature? Hmm . . . that sounds a lot like traditional medicine! In āyurveda and Elemental-Wellness, we talk about poop because it is such an accessible and noninvasive indication of how the "system" is running, if you will.

Generally speaking, it's a sign of healthy digestion when you have one regular, well-formed bowel movement in the morning. This has a great deal to do with the daily rhythm (or dinacarya, also spelled dinacharya), which corresponds to what we now call the 24-hour daily cycle, or circadian rhythm. Historically it was believed that a single day consisted of three cycles, each lasting 4 hours, that repeated in a 12-hour cycle. We'll circle back to these in Chapter 7.

When bowel movements are frequent, loose, smelly, oily, or smeary, these signify an imbalance of incomplete digestion. What could be causing this? The main culprits are diet and activity, along with misalignment with daily rhythms. Dietary causes of loose stools could be an excess of raw or fibrous foods, overly spicy foods, or fried/greasy fast foods. Activity causes could be eating mindlessly, so that food is not properly chewed, processed, or digested; or eating large meals and snacks at the wrong times of the day, such as close to bedtime. Incompatible food combinations can also cause irregular digestion, incomplete absorption of nutrients, and excess or poorly-formed stools.

Potential solutions to pacify a pitta imbalance include nutrition and timing or rhythm. Instead of consuming hot, spicy, acidic, raw, or rough foods that are difficult to digest (excess Fire), think of the opposite elements to balance: Earth and Space. Consider grounding foods like whole grains, lean proteins, milder seasonings, and lightly roasted vegetables or stews that are easier to digest, as they are already broken down a bit by the process of heating and cooking with plant-based oils (coconut, sesame, avocado). Likewise, you might choose foods that have more Space Element: subtle spices that assist digestion (cumin, coriander, fennel) and lighter, smaller meal portions until your system rebalances and regulates.

As for timing and rhythm (I love the musical references here—after all, your digestion is a fine-tuned instrument!), it's ideal to make breakfast a warm meal that gives you energy until lunchtime, somewhere between late morning and early afternoon, at which time it's best to enjoy your largest, heaviest meal that sustains and satisfies you until the early evening. Your digestive fire is at its strongest at the same time that the sun is at its peak around midday, making it the best time to consume more difficult-to-digest foods, like meats, cheese, and dairy, that take more time and energy. (Hint: this is the best time to indulge in dessert.)

By late afternoon or evening, a smaller dinner works best when it's consumed at least a few hours before bedtime. This gives your digestive system ample time to process and assimilate nutrients prior to going to sleep. Once you're asleep, your body is engineered to spend more time resting, recovering, and detoxifying. If you eat too close to bedtime, you may experience heartburn or reflux, or wake up with a "brick belly." Ironically, eating too close to bedtime may cause you to wake up feeling even more hungry than usual! This is because you have confused your system. Rather than allowing all your vital organs to do their job of detoxifying and balancing, you've called the blood back to the stomach and intestines to process your television-watching munchies (chips, cookies, ice cream) or, worse yet, your midnight snacks (getting up in the middle of the night to eat??—this is a combined eating and sleeping disorder).

The brick feeling (kapha imbalance, or too much Earth) is just a symptom of food not being transformed into nutrients that can benefit the body, but instead being diverted directly to elimination through the colon. What's the antidote to brick belly kapha imbalance? As always, like increases like, and opposites balance. Large, heavy Earth stools in the rectum can be "rectified" by seeking the opposite: Air and Space Elements. Choose foods that are lighter, such as steamed vegetables, leafy greens, and produce that contains more space than sugar and starch, such as broccoli or raw salads instead of baked sweet potatoes and corn. Regarding activity, rev up your metabolism with a brisk walk after lunch or dinner to get things moving, and start your day with some simple stretches and twists that open your torso and massage your organs of digestion and elimination, helping them to function optimally.

What if your problem is gas, bloating, or constipation? These are signs of vāta imbalance, or excesses of Air and Space Elements. In that case, you'd want to choose the opposite—more Earth and Water foods. Moist rice and vegetables roasted or sauteed with sesame oil or lightly tossed with olive oil can be helpful. Eating dry popcorn, chips, crunchy granola cereals, rough/raw vegetables, salads that are difficult to digest, and flatulence-producing foods such as large beans will aggravate an already overly gassy system.

What if you say your diet and nutrition are textbook perfect but you still suffer with dry, scant, irregular bowel movements or uncomfortable bloating? Could it be a lifestyle or activity imbalance? Are you getting enough sleep (seven to eight hours of quality sleep)? Are you running around ragged from one thing to the next without honoring the cycles of the day? Have you been traveling (excess movement in a car, plane, train, bus) or changing time zones? Have you simply been running crazily to work and carpooling to one event after another, perhaps eating meals on the fly while in the car, or not at all?

That's too much Wind and movement! Excess Wind not only blows up the belly like a balloon, but it also dries up the stool, causing difficult elimination and scanty, hard poop. (Again, what do you notice when you pick up after your dog's business? Similarly, what do you notice when a baby is off her schedule and ends up gassy and fussy?) How can you expect your digestion to keep up?

The answer is to slow down, to sit down, and eat a healthy meal without watching television, without checking emails or messages or social media. Eat mindfully, even silently, for at least one meal per day. Beginning the day with a silent breakfast can allow you to experience the flavors, colors, and textures of your food, to appreciate with gratitude what it took for the food to appear in front of you. (Think: Who planted, cultivated, harvested, transported, and packaged your food before it ever made it to your grocery cart or kitchen?) You'll likely find that you enjoy your food more when you take the time to eat mindfully. And the by-product, so to speak, will be more smooth and comfortable digestion.

The beautiful thing about āyurveda and Elemental-Wellness is that they *are* common sense. Rather than reinventing the wheel or disregarding Western knowledge, you can combine modern medicine with traditional wisdom to enhance your own wellness, as well as be a more holistic health care provider for your patients who rely on you for their own wellness.

Points to Ponder

- How has your digestion been over the past three months?
- What is the quality of your bowel movements?
- How might you enjoy improved digestion through modifying either your diet or activities?
- What is one small tweak you can commit to for the next three weeks?
- How might you incorporate inquiry (by reviewing their medical histories and chief concerns, for example) and knowledge of your patients' digestion and elimination to better understand their overall health?
- How might a holistic approach enhance the level of care you provide for your patients?

■ ■ ■

Caregiving and Codependence

What makes some health care providers appear to be so resilient and blissful, while many others are so prone to burnout? Perhaps it has to do with how some of us came to choose helping professions in the first place. I used to think I knew what the term codependency meant. That is, until I read author Melody Beattie's classic and groundbreaking book *Codependent No More*.

Codependency encompasses a spectrum of behaviors that are usually learned at a young age, typically the formative years from birth to seven years old, but can also be learned later in life. These behaviors include: repressing or denying the appropriate expression of one's true feelings, communicating indirectly (not speaking truthfully and directly to someone in favor of complaining about them to someone else), trying to be perfect or being a "failure" (these are opposite expressions of the same feeling of being unworthy of love), and taking everything personally.

With codependency, you learn ways to stay safe and navigate your world. You likely attempt to "fix" or *rescue* others, to control their behavior, to protect them from the consequences of their self-destructive behaviors, and to protect them from their own feelings/fears/insecurities/discomforts and experiences. You are eager to jump in and *help* others (=rescue), because you are a helpful, compassionate, and loving person, and also because it makes you feel more comfortable, safe, and lovable when everyone is happy and well. You are "taught" by your primary influences, usually a parent or caregiver, through:

- Explicit instructions: "Do not raise your voice at me!" = deny/repress your true feelings.
- Implied rules: Being a "good" boy or girl makes you lovable.
- Modeling behavior: The parent or caregiver either violates their own rules by having a shouting or crying tantrum, or by pretending that someone else's unacceptable behavior doesn't exist, and thereby "sweeps it under the carpet" or otherwise ignores it.

Jan is a retired psychiatrist. Here is her story.

When I recall my greatest work stressors, the common denominator was intentional violence by a patient on staff and sometimes against other patients. There were several sociopaths who had extensive histories of violence and also had mental illness.

When police would come to investigate incidents, they would take the providers' statements, but the DA wouldn't prosecute because he said, "Well, the person has a mental illness." But when I asked the patient who had attacked and injured others why they had done so, they replied, "Because I felt like it" or "To see if I could [get away with it before staff could intervene]."

Some attacks were, without a doubt, intentional, preplanned, and calculated. My efforts to involve a newer administration in finding solutions in how to manage a handful of these sociopaths were rejected, dismissed, or even ridiculed. After years of the new medical director being unresponsive and unwilling to help me to keep my staff and other patients safe from the very few patients who'd plot to intentionally injure others, I finally decided I had to leave. I retired early.

Jan may or may not have grown up in a codependent household where there were addictions and/or abuses, but she certainly chose a profession in which she was helping others, frequently having to rescue others, and being told by multiple authorities (law enforcement and her direct supervisor) that she should ignore her own needs for safety in favor of caring for the patients. The stresses contributed to a diet of junk food and unhealthy weight gain. She didn't have much time to get together with friends very often, and her social circle outside of work was very limited.

Sadly, Jan had put herself aside (through her own choices and by allowing others to do so) to the point where the best way to take care of herself was to retire early.

The good news is that she now enjoys nutritious foods, reading, gardening, hobbies, and socializing with friends. Jan feels much healthier. Sometimes the best solution to being in a toxic environment is to remove yourself, quit, or retire. My hope is that, with heightened self-awareness and the tools in this book, you are able to practice preventive self-care *before* your environment becomes unhealthy, or that you can identify earlier when things become imbalanced so that you can course correct and perhaps find a healthier way to continue in your health care role.

Melody Beattie further explains how "after so many years of rescuing our patients—giving so much and receiving far less in return—many professional helpers adopt a hostile attitude toward their clients (patients). When we take care of people and do things we don't want to do, we ignore personal needs, wants, and feelings. We put *ourselves* aside."

Does this sound familiar? You're "gowned up" or "scrubbed in," so you must ignore your needs to nourish and hydrate yourself, to relieve yourself in the bathroom, and to rest your neck/back/eyes/etc. The patient becomes the most important person in the moment, despite what might be happening in your personal life. I'm not saying that the patient *shouldn't* be the focus. What I am saying is that you can become more aware of how you are caring for yourself and your own needs. Do you take a lunch break? If you do, what do you do with it? Is it glorified admin time? Do you nosh on junk food or scroll through social media/news/other people's drama? Or do you eat a nourishing meal as mindfully as possible? Do you take a break from screens, if only to briefly enjoy your meal? Do you get outside for a walk and some fresh air, or at least enjoy a change of scenery?

Health care providers are at a high risk of burnout precisely because of the work that we do, and the way that we deliver care. If you are even more likely to overcare, overfix, and over-rescue because of codependent behaviors that you picked up either early on or later in life, it may be time for some introspection and self-inquiry.

■ ■ ■

What About Conflicts, Compassion, and Communication?

As health care providers, we can assume that we are all compassionate to some degree—or at least I hope so! I remember an exercise early in my dental school training. We had actor "patients" who presented with unique medical histories, and our task was to interview them and review their histories. In hindsight, I believe the intention was to hone our skills in compassion and connection. Interestingly, I received feedback from one of the patients that I should be careful about how caring I am.

Really? This stuck with me for decades as a bit of a strange juxtaposition. Aren't we supposed to care?

Fast forward, I had enrolled in a training designed to help leaders facilitate group dynamics. The embodiment of learning required that we experience firsthand some of the exercises that we would potentially include in our future workshops. As such, we practiced multiple exercises throughout the weeks of learning.

One of them involved a simple (or so I thought!) partner exercise in which we lined up against a wall with our partner facing us about 12 feet away. I was immediately concerned about others' vulnerability—the expression "back up against a wall" has very strong connotations, and images of firing squads and mug shots flooded my brain. For myself, my mind immediately went to elementary school lunchtime recess in second grade, where we played dodgeball. I was good at dodgeball and it was fun!

This was meant to be a physical demonstration of a verbal technique for addressing aggressive or unwelcome behavior. It leaned into the martial art of aikido, with which I was familiar, as my son had studied aikido and my coach had been a black belt instructor of aikido. Okay, great! It's time to play. Or so I thought.

As the facilitators demonstrated the exercise, the female instructor pretended to run at the male instructor in anger with her fists clenched, arms flailing, and jaw tight. The male instructor demonstrated this technique:

1. Step aside.
2. Connect (by gently but firmly grasping the aggressor's arm).
3. Redirect in the opposite direction (kind of a do-si-do turn technique).

As they repeated the demonstration, I said aloud, "Oh, just let her run into the wall," and I heard the whole room erupt into laughter at my playful attempt at humor. One second later, my gaze returned to my partner, and she was not laughing! In fact, she had a stony death stare, directed straight at me! Thinking she was joking in return, I said, "What's the matter? I was joking."

She responded, "Now I can't trust you. I don't feel safe. I need to take care of myself, and I'm not doing the exercise."

Whaaat? I felt confused, and then I realized she wasn't kidding, that somehow my joke felt triggering to her. As a compassionate person, I apologized and tried to reassure her that I would never intentionally hurt her, and that she was safe with me—I would not allow her to be hurt. She resisted and persisted that she did not feel safe. Finally, she agreed that we could continue with the exercise as long as we went ver-rry slowly. Okay, great. So she pretended to approach me with what I thought was a laughable attempt at aggression. True to my word and to the exercise, I stepped aside, connected with her arm/elbow, and redirected her in the opposite direction.

Now it was time to switch roles, and at this point I didn't even want to play. We went through the motions, and then it was time to come back to the circle and continue with the workshop. As fate would have it, my partner and I were seated directly adjacent to each other, and the facilitators were not in my direct line of vision. As I rejoined the group, I could feel my body temperature rising, my heart racing, and my eyes welling up with tears. My nose became congested as tears streamed silently down my face, and I was aware of my body language as I held my hand against my face in a physical barrier between me and my recent partner. I completely shut down and stopped participating.

What's wrong with me? I silently queried. *Why am I so upset, and why can't I get my shit together?*

I was aware that even though the facilitators couldn't see my expression or body language from where I was seated, other participants could see me and my obvious change in energy and presence. I weighed the options of excusing myself from the group (would that draw even more unwanted attention and disruption?) versus staying and collecting myself. The waves washed over me, and I recalled a basic concept: *When feelings seem really big and overwhelming, it's likely about something else. When had I felt like this before, particularly in my formative years before the age of seven?*

And then it hit me. While my partner had felt triggered by my attempt at humor, *I* felt triggered by her reaction and stony stare. I realized that I was four or five years old again. My mother never hit me or yelled at me, but oh-my-goodness that look! I knew I was in trouble, and *I was full of shame.* I felt confused, misunderstood, and hurt. I desperately wanted to be loved and understood. As I sat in the circle, I wrote down these feelings and insights in order to take care of myself, and when it was finally time for our lunch break, I couldn't wait to leave! I needed time and space outdoors in nature, to take care of myself, to ground myself, to process the morning's events.

The happy ending to the story is that my partner and I talked after the session. She had begun to spin a tale that I wasn't acknowledging her feelings/experience, which was the furthest thing from the truth. In fact, I jumped to the rescue, wanting to fix her and the situation, feeling terrible for inadvertently hurting her, and wanting to make it better for the both of us. With her permission, I shared my experience of being triggered by her reaction to being triggered.

Whaaat? You can't make this stuff up!

We acknowledged each other and "made up." I went outdoors for a walk/hike/jog in nature to take care of myself before lunch. I let the facilitators know what had happened and that my partner and I had cleared things between us. They assisted me in further processing the experience. And there was more to learn.

What were the lessons? While I had initially thought this would be a fluffy, playful exercise, you never know what can be triggering to another person! Should we soften all the edges so that we never offend anyone? I don't think so. If we remove any potential irritant or offense, we just might end up with the equivalent of milk toast—a boring, whitewashed, sterile existence devoid of passion and energy.

But again, what are the lessons? First of all, I realized that I had failed at the whole object of the exercise! In my attempt to be caring and compassionate, and "right" a perceived "wrong," I had forgotten the first step in the facilitator's demonstration: to step aside. My partner's reaction actually had nothing to do with me. I jumped into making amends—a residual codependent behavior that served me at one time in my life but no longer serves. While my self-purported purpose is to "lift others up so that they may empower themselves," I realized that my rushing in to rescue her was an attempt at control and was completely disempowering to my partner. It was a way for me to feel better about myself.

What would have been healthier for myself and more supportive of my partner would have been for me to *step aside*—to not take her reaction personally, and to witness and observe her experience so that I could support her to empower herself. I could have asked her what was going on for her, what she needed to do to take care of herself, whether she needed professional intervention, and how I might support her. Not taking things personally would have minimized my own triggering reaction. I could have taken better care of myself, interrupted the flood of emotions, and stayed present for my partner. Then I could have helped her to redirect her behavior, and we both could have returned to the group feeling safe, grounded, and intact.

I later realized that the same holds true for our patients. As a dentist, I am acutely aware of any sights (noting the visible needles/instruments when a patient enters the operatory), sounds (playing calming music in the background and drowning out potentially irritating sounds and distracting conversations), smells (having pleasant aromas throughout the office as opposed to a dirty bathroom or overly antiseptic odors), and touches (asking permission before touching a patient, and being gentle and aware of their individual sensitivities). This is what I'm trained to do, and I pride myself for doing it well. As a yoga instructor, I carry the same responsibilities: to offer options, opt-outs, modifications, safety, and pleasing aromas/lights/music; and to not touch students without explicit consent. In the end, anyone can be triggered by anything at any moment! We simply do not and cannot control another individual's entire experience.

As a health care provider, it is much more empowering to recognize when a patient is nervous or upset and remain curious and supportive, rather than jumping in to "fix" them, which is completely disempowering. If a dental patient presents for an appointment and is visibly anxious, I can help them to help themselves by coaching them to become more embodied.

Breath is the first and most accessible tool. I guide my patients to exhale completely and then allow the next inhalation to happen naturally. When I see clenched fists or furrowed eyebrows, I invite them to release tension in their hands and face and invite ease. We practice slow belly breathing together—this allows both my patient and me to ground and be present. If they are open, and with their permission, I can guide them in a centering embodiment practice of noticing *where* they feel stress/tension in their body, *what* it *feels* like, and whether the feeling has *shape/texture*, as well as asking them: *If the feeling had a voice, what would it say?* This helps the individual to become more grounded and embodied so their sympathetic fight-or-flight response doesn't become all-consuming or overwhelming. If we can avert a crisis in the dental chair, I'm all for it!

From there, I can guide the patient to identify another part of their body that is feeling opposite or "not that." Again, they can notice the location, feeling, shape, and texture of their stress, and determine whether it has a voice. They can toggle between the two sensations and then meld them into one experience, noticing how they feel and what happens for them. The intention is for the patient to identify a safe anchor that they already possess within themselves. If a history of trauma is revealed or the patient is in need of additional help, then we can make a referral to appropriate resources, just as we would make a referral for any other procedure that warrants a colleague's/specialist's services.

Would it be easier to just sedate them? Possibly, and yet it wouldn't be empowering, because they wouldn't have tapped into their own strength and they'd probably need the sedation again the next time. Sometimes people *do* need sedation, and sometimes they just need someone with the skills and patience to support them.

You may be thinking, "I haven't got time for that!" or "That's not my job! I don't get paid to be a therapist." Those may be true statements for you, and if that is the case, then I implore you to honor what is within your wheelhouse and have the discernment to know if and when it's appropriate for you to lead this exercise.

Learning how to facilitate a workshop is completely different from being a health care provider, right? Maybe not. One of my insights is that each patient encounter and every human interaction has the potential to be transformational. Understanding how to manage unwanted aggressive behavior is a valuable life skill. Within one week of learning these techniques, we experienced the following "situation" in my dental practice.

We were still in the process of hiring a new hygienist, and in the meantime we were working with part-time help and temporary hygienists while interviewing potential candidates. In addition to my other duties, I was cleaning a lot of teeth! During our morning meeting, we discussed that "Marilyn" was coming in at noon for her regular hygiene visit, and she was very anxious and phobic. We informed the temporary hygienist "Kristen" (who had worked with us on numerous occasions and whom we would have hired except that she wasn't able to commit to regular hours) that Marilyn would request the overhead lights to be off, the music to be turned down, and the X-ray shield to be draped over her like a weighted blanket the whole time. She'd then want to dash out at the end of her appointment without stopping at the front desk. No problem.

When Kristen went to the reception room to invite Marilyn in for her appointment, Marilyn immediately attacked her in front of the other patients. "I don't know you. I wasn't expecting you. Are you just out of school? Where's the other girl?" Despite Kristen's best attempts to diffuse the situation and reassure the patient, Marilyn remained visibly upset, angry, and scared. Kristen and another long-term team member entered Marilyn's world and gently guided her, enabling her to calm down and come back to the hygienist's operatory. My team members came to me, explained the situation, and asked for help. It was another example of being triggered. Clearly Marilyn had a history of fear and likely trauma that contributed to her extreme reaction and behavior. It wasn't our job to fix that in a few minutes. What was my task at the moment was to step aside, connect, and redirect.

I sat with Marilyn, and acknowledged and listened to her concerns. We breathed together. Then I connected by clarifying the situation—that the previous hygienist had left (so that was not an option), that we had been very selective with who worked in our office, and that we'd been working a lot with Kristen, who was very qualified. I asked whether she would be comfortable staying at that point, and she agreed. Kristen came back, we smoothed everything over, and they completed the appointment, albeit not without Marilyn complaining that Kristen was poking her when she didn't even have any instruments in her hands. At the end of the appointment, I went in to review Marilyn's exam. She complimented Kristen, asked me to thank her, and apologized for her behavior. Then, true to form, she dashed out of the office without stopping at the front desk.

As a leader and team member, however, my work was not done. I could see that Kristen was upset, and we sat down privately to talk before lunchtime. Through tears, Kristen sobbed that she considers herself to be compassionate and an empath, so it was extremely upsetting to experience being attacked in front of the other patients. She apologized for crying in the office. Obviously, Marilyn had been triggered and then her reaction was triggering for Kristen.

Hmm . . . didn't this sound familiar? I asked Kristen if she could identify another time when she had felt this way. Without sharing specifics, she said that she could recall more than one incident. With Kristen's permission, I shared my experience of saying something that was triggering and sub-sequently being triggered at the workshop as an example. She exhaled and said that the experience gave her some things to reflect upon personally at another time.

Emphasizing that she hadn't done anything wrong and that the patient's behavior had nothing to do with her as a person or as a hygienist, I talked to Kristen about what she needed in order to take care of herself and what support she needed from me. We both agreed that we needed to eat lunch and get some fresh air, and Kristen thanked me for being a compassionate human. At the end of the day, we gave our weekly delivery of fresh office flowers to Kristen as a token of appreciation and caring, and she was so appreciative.

In hindsight, it would have been more ideal if a familiar team member had introduced the unfamiliar hygienist to the fearful patient, and that was a nuance that we brought to our morning meeting for future improvements. In any event, conflicts are bound to happen. How we manage conflict, the way we communicate, and the compassion that we express help to tip the balance toward *Bliss, Not Burnout.*

Health care providers have a Hippocratic obligation to "do no harm." That includes providing an environment that is safe—physically, mentally, and emotionally. That being said, it is impossible to prevent our patients (or even our team members!) from having their own experiences—we simply can't protect people from themselves and their own inner experience. As with training in CPR and basic life support, the goal is to be skilled enough to manage whatever situation arises, at least until additional support is available. The same holds true in a dental office as well as any other health care setting. The take-home message, as with any offering as you continue reading here, is that if a suggestion seems useful or interesting to you, consider trying it out. If it doesn't, let it go. As Bruce Lee said about his martial arts training, "Absorb what is useful." Not every exercise or idea is going to be useful to everyone, and that's the wonderful thing that makes us uniquely beautiful beings.

Points to Ponder

- Regarding communication, what skills do you have in caring for patients who may feel anxious, scared, angry, or triggered?
- How might you better serve yourself and your patients by practicing slow belly breathing together?

7

"D" IS FOR "DAILY" (DINACARYA) AND DIET

In Sanskrit, the word "dinacarya" refers to your daily practices/conduct/observances. Loosely you can translate it as your "daily routines." At this point, it may come as no surprise that āyurveda and Elemental-Wellness view the daily cycle, or circadian rhythm, through the lens of the Five Great Elements and the three doshas. Basically, each dosha dominates a four-hour time frame twice a day. You can visualize this on an analog clock face:

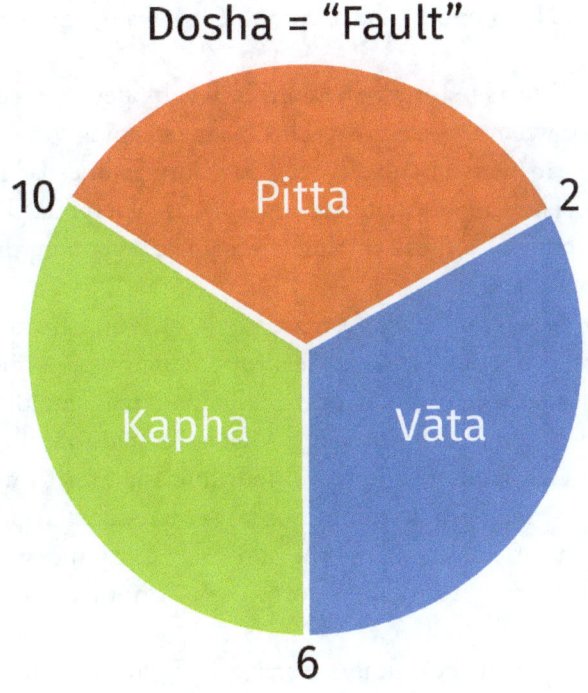

Dosha = "Fault"

Early Morning Vāta

Your ideal day begins toward the end of the first vāta cycle, which occurs roughly from 2:00 a.m. to 6:00 a.m. Since this is vāta dosha, the elements of Air and Space predominate. You may experience this as increased rapid eye movement (REM) or dream sleep during these hours. Traditionally it was considered to be a time that was more spiritual, a realm between lucidity and death, when the subconscious mind dominated brain activity.

With the stresses of modern daily life, you may experience morning vāta as a time of insomnia, either with sleep maintenance or resumption. It's the time when you wake in the middle of the night, purportedly to void, and then you can't get back to sleep because your mind is busy and restless. Yogis describe this active mind state as "monkey mind," akin to a busy monkey who is screeching incessantly and moving restlessly and relentlessly. In Chapter 5, I shared some grounding breathing techniques that can be helpful to settle a busy mind.

If you find yourself overly awake for more than 20 to 30 minutes in the middle of the night, it's best to get out of bed. While keeping the lights dim, you can do some gentle tension-relieving stretches or light, mindless activity, such as folding laundry or emptying the dishwasher. Another useful strategy is reading something written on paper, or at least using blue blocking glasses if you're reading from a screen. Any artificial light from a computer, television, or smartphone can signal your suprachiasmatic nucleus in your brain's hypothalamus that it's time to wake up! Once you've read or folded long enough to become sleepy again, you can return to bed to resume sleep.

For thousands of years before we had artificial light, people went to sleep when it was dark and got up when the sun rose. This meant sleeping longer during cold and dark times of the year (winter) and sleeping less during times of increased daytime sunlight (summer). They ate enough breakfast to last energetically until lunchtime. Farmers are still in tune with these rhythms of nature, beginning their workday early to tend to their crops and animals.

To harness the potential of vāta on a daily basis, you can rise in the morning before the sun rises. This subtle time is ideal for meditation and quiet reflection. For some individuals, it's an ideal time to pray. Other activities could be reading uplifting or inspirational material and journaling. One colleague found that 4:30 a.m. was the perfect quietly creative and uninterrupted time for him to write a book! You might benefit from some light stretching or yoga to awaken your body and mind, or you could enjoy a reflective walk as the sun rises. Early morning is also a lovely time to enjoy a warm drink, whether it's coffee, tea, or hot lemon water, to stimulate elimination.

In contrast, vāta is *not* the best time to engage in vigorous or strenuous activities— your body was simply not made to wake up and jump into action like a firefighter at

3:00 a.m.! As a certified yoga instructor, I used to teach an early morning yoga class that I called Wake Up Wednesdays at a studio in my community. My class began at 6:15 a.m. with sunbreaths and a brief centering while setting a theme or intention for the practice. I guided students to gradually invite movement into their physical bodies through warm-ups and gentle flows, with the option to increase effort and challenge along the way. Incorporating breathwork throughout each session and concluding with Savasana deep relaxation provided an opportunity to integrate the experience. By 7:15 a.m. each Wednesday, both the students and I felt awake, centered, focused, joyful, and ready to take on the challenges of the day!

Morning Kapha

Kapha follows vāta in the daily cycle, roughly from 6:00 a.m. to 10:00 a.m. Since kapha dosha comprises primarily Earth and Water Elements, morning is a time for building your day and beginning the bulk of your daily work. If you like to lift weights or strength train, or to take long hikes that require endurance and stamina, this is an ideal time to do so. After enjoying enough breakfast to last energetically until lunchtime, you'll be ready to tackle whatever challenges arise. Eating a light breakfast is like lighting kindling to grow a bigger fire: it starts slow, light and subtle, before building to heat and vigor. Morning is an excellent time to address your biggest challenges, including the things that you might want to postpone or put off for another day (read: procrastination!) because it's when you can do your heaviest lifting not only physically, but mentally. Are you working on a project or presentation? You may find morning work to be the most productive time of day.

In my dental practice, we generally prefer to reserve time for the more challenging appointments in the morning when we have the most energy and stamina to focus for sustained periods of time, and schedule routine follow-up and shorter appointments in the afternoon. Likewise, most non-emergent surgical and operating room procedures are scheduled in the morning to allow not only the time necessary for complex cases, but also to harness the surgeon's greatest capacity to perform optimally.

You might have noticed that when you oversleep, you can actually end up feeling more groggy than rested. This is in part due to missing the transition from subtle vāta to nourishing and building kapha. If you rise in the middle of morning kapha, you may need more morning coffee! Your body can feel heavier and lethargic, and your mind can take longer to wake up and feel alert. It may be difficult to focus or gather momentum to address your day.

Now this is fine when it's a choice once in a while—I'm not advocating that you adhere to a rigid schedule 24/7. What I *am* saying is that when you do choose to sleep in, you'll have a better understanding of what to expect and why you feel as you do. I choose to sleep in sometimes, too. On the other hand, I also like to get up at roughly the same time on my days off as I do during my work week in order to feel my best and to experience better sleep hygiene. Your body and mind are at their best when you keep the same schedule; it's easier to fall asleep, maintain restful sleep, and wake up feeling refreshed, often before the alarm goes off! For those who work third shift, studies show that it's actually beneficial to try to keep the same eating schedule as you would if you worked the first shift. That could look like eating dinner before your evening shift, bringing a lighter snack to eat overnight, and eating breakfast at the conclusion of your shift before going to sleep. Eating a meal less than two to three hours before going to sleep is not ideal digestively, but it's better than eating a big meal in the middle of the night.

As you can imagine (and maybe you've experienced), alternating shift work is even more problematic than working the third shift. When my daughter was working as an emergency department technician while applying to physician assistant programs, her 12-and-a-half-hour shifts would change between night and day every third week. Typically, it would take several days to adjust to the "time change," which is even more detrimental than changing time zones. While working from 7:00 p.m. to 7:30 a.m. (did I mention that the commute could be as much as 45 minutes each way?), she tried to maintain that schedule even on her days off. What do you do by yourself in the middle of the night when everyone else in your apartment is asleep? There's only so much reading or Netflix or internet surfing you can do in the wee hours, and invariably her sleep was disjointed and interrupted. It wasn't until later when she started PA school that she realized just how sleep deprived she had been the entire 10 months. "Mom, I've been running on a sleep deficit for so long, and I didn't even appreciate just how exhausted I was becoming," she told me. Despite the long hours and rigorous challenges of her PA program, the more regular hours and sleep schedule made a huge difference in her wellness.

Midday Pitta

Roughly around mid-to-late morning, morning kapha transitions into midday pitta. This is the time when the sun is at its brightest, hottest peak in the sky, and it is also when the Fire Element of pitta burns brightest (with a lesser influence of Water Element as well). Late morning to early afternoon is when your digestive Fire is also at its peak, which is why it's the best time to enjoy your biggest meal. Foods that are heavier and perhaps harder to digest, such as meats, cheese, and fats, can best be digested when consumed midday. First, as already mentioned, your digestion is programmed to work hardest at this time of day, and second, you have many more waking, primarily upright hours to digest and process anything complex. So go ahead and enjoy dessert with lunch!

While you might think that having a light salad for lunch is a good way to watch your caloric intake and your figure, you might also find yourself in an energy slump and craving a sugary snack or caffeine right around 3:00 p.m. to 4:00 p.m. because your light lunch wasn't enough food to fuel you all the way to your evening meal. If you're a snacker or grazer, or have the habit of eating four to five smaller meals, this may sound familiar, and if you need to observe a particular dietary schedule for medical reasons, by all means, do so!

But generally speaking, the traditional approach is that when you snack and graze, your body isn't finished digesting the first meal before being challenged with another meal. Your body may be in a different phase of digestion, and you may find that your food doesn't digest as well. This shows up as signs of indigestion—burping, farting, bloating, brick belly, loose or sticky stools, or acid reflux—and generally not assimilating the nutrients from your food. This is basically a waste of food if you're just putting it in one end (your mouth) and it's passing out the other end largely unchanged or only half-digested. Another sign of incomplete digestion is when your energy depletes quickly or you get hungry again hours before your next mealtime. If you're in the habit of snacking, skipping meals, or having a light lunch and a big evening meal, try transitioning to a larger lunch meal and see how it goes for you. You may be pleasantly surprised!

As for physical and mental activities, midday pitta is ideally suited to problem solve and wrap up the larger projects you started in the morning. Since pitta qualities include sharp, piercing, spreading, hot, and transformational, you can harness these qualities into a disciplined focus to complete the tasks that you started, as well as keep your vision clear and intentional as you segue into the afternoon. While morning kapha is useful to do the building and heavy lifting, midday pitta is necessary to keep things on track and moving in the desired direction, so you don't get bogged down with the weight of kapha's Earth and Water. Pitta's Fire burns through late-morning fog and inertia so that you stay on course.

After your midday meal/lunch while pitta is busy digesting your food, it can be helpful to take a little walk around the neighborhood to keep things moving and blood flowing. Very vigorous exercise is not advised, as it can direct blood flow to the large muscles of your extremities and divert blood away from the organs of digestion. In many cultures, lunch is the main meal of the day, and it is taken leisurely with family and friends. A little catnap or siesta of 20 to 30 minutes can revive your energy for the afternoon. In the real world, this isn't always realistic or remotely possible, but you can improvise:

- One dentist colleague routinely schedules a longer lunch break so he has time to take a walk in a local park. When the weather isn't conducive to walking, he'll set an alarm and take a nap in his car to refresh himself for the afternoon.
- When I was pregnant, I'd regularly rest in one of my dental patient chairs after lunch, which was also an opportunity to elevate my feet.

- You can fold your arms to make a pillow and lay your head on your desk to rest, even if sleep doesn't happen.
- Simply closing your eyes or covering them with the cupped palms of your hands for a minute can help restore your vision and relieve eye fatigue.
- Being in nature is helpful to soothe pretty much any dosha. If you can't get outside due to work demands, try to get near a window so you can look outside from time to time or for a few minutes when you get a break.

Afternoon Vāta

We've discussed how the doshas come into play for the first 12 hours of the day. During the second half of the day, the doshas repeat in sequence with slightly different emphasis. Following midday pitta, afternoon vāta envelopes the remainder of the afternoon. Again, the vāta elements of Air and Space are in play, with the qualities of being light, clear, subtle, cool, dry, rough, and especially mobile. Although ideally you won't be asleep dreaming, the middle of the afternoon is the ideal time to stay awake and daydream! This is when vāta potential can shine: artistry, brainstorming, and creativity. It's the perfect time for group meetings and collaboration. Instead of allowing your energy to plummet, afternoon is the perfect time to reboot momentum and energize teamwork. Your enthusiasm and excitement can synergize momentum with others. Ideas are subtle and intangible, and all thoughts and electrical nerve conduction are considered to be vāta energy. It could be a time to do creative writing, design a presentation, or meet with colleagues to develop action plans for future endeavors.

Maybe you're starting to feel hungry or sluggish despite eating a nourishing lunch. Rather than reach for a candy bar or heavy, processed snacks from a vending machine, you might benefit from a lighter, crunchier snack, like a crispy apple, fresh carrot sticks, or some popcorn to carry you over until your evening meal. Anything heavier could actually weigh you down, cause you to feel sleepy, and interfere with you enjoying your evening meal.

And what about physical activity? As much as I advocate yoga and exercise, going on a very long run or participating in a hot or power yoga class may leave you feeling depleted rather than de-stressed. In contrast, late afternoon can be a great time for a moderate jog, bike ride, or brisk walk to alleviate the stresses of the day and prepare for winding down. Likewise, a Vinyasa flow or a moderate yoga class that releases tension and promotes relaxation is useful toward late afternoon/early evening, before your evening meal. If you don't have time or interest in moving in the afternoon, movement can look like playing with your pets or children, or doing some light gardening. Each of these activities facilitates taking the potentially swirling energy of late afternoon and funneling it down like a centrifuge so you can transition into evening and wind down from the day's activities.

Evening Kapha

Sometime around 6:00 p.m., afternoon vāta transitions into evening kapha. While traditionally kapha is considered to span 6:00 p.m. to 10:00 p.m., depending on many factors (work schedule, stage in life, even how east-versus-west you're living within your particular time zone!), kapha may start and end a bit earlier or later for you. Whereas morning kapha is a time of building and heavy lifting, evening kapha is a time to embrace the restorative, nurturing qualities of Earth and Water.

Your evening meal is ideally light to moderate in both portion size and heaviness. Instead of mashed potatoes, gravy, red meat, lots of buttered or starchy vegetables, followed with cheesecake or a dairy-based dessert like ice cream, you might find it easier to digest leaner proteins, simple grains (like quinoa or rice), and vegetables that are roasted or sauteed in plant-based oils like coconut, sesame, sunflower, olive, or avocado. Dessert is best enjoyed at lunchtime when you have plenty of time and a strong digestive Fire to process it.

Your evening meal plan can be as simple as a smaller portion size of the same kinds of foods that you eat during your midday meal. More importantly, food is meant to be enjoyed. You can certainly eat mashed potatoes, gravy, and roast beef at 8:00 p.m.— I'm not advocating rigidity here! And you also might notice that when you do indulge in steak and potatoes at night, you feel like you have a brick belly (or "food baby!") in the morning, because it was too difficult to digest a heavy meal so late in the day.

Again, it's all about mindfulness and awareness of choices. Eating a heavy evening meal on occasion is probably not going to be a big deal. Eating a late heavy meal most days of the week could pose a problem with indigestion, compromised sleep quality, and unhealthy weight gain.

Generally speaking, preparing and eating your evening meal doesn't take four hours, so what else happens during evening kapha? That's where the nurturing and restorative aspects come into play. Evening is the time to wind down. In fact, sleep hygiene and bedtime routine ideally begin hours before your head hits the pillow. If you've ever been a parent or caregiver for small children, you know how important this routine can be! You know the value of transitioning from the flurry of activity (or from the energy of school or daycare) to a calmer environment at home.

From the time my children were babies, our evening routine involved eating our meal together. As soon as they could stand on a chair or stool to reach the counter, they began helping with meal preparation from time to time. We would say a version of grace (mindfully acknowledging and being thankful for our food) and take turns going around the table sharing three things for which we were grateful. After dinner, we'd clean up and I'd wrap up any homework with my school-aged children. Bedtime always involved a bath and then reading books together and singing a song before tucking them in. Of course, every night wasn't perfect—there were definitely nights of pure chaos! But this bedtime routine served them well for a good night's sleep.

In the same way, adults benefit from a solid bedtime routine. Give yourself the gift of transitioning from your work life to your home life. This could look like stopping at the gym after work to exercise, pausing on your commute to walk in a local park or just sit and look at nature, or taking a few minutes for yourself to breathe and "be" before you open the door to your home. If you have time, playing with children or pets; chatting with a friend, neighbor, or family member (even by phone); gardening; playing or listening to music; or taking a warm shower or bath before you eat are all beautiful ways to transition from work to home life.

Ideally, you take time to mindfully prepare your evening meal. Think **FLOSS**: **F**resh, **L**ocal, **O**rganic, **S**easonal, **S**ustainable for the majority of your meals. Sometimes the most mindful thing is remembering to swing through the drive-through window at a fast food establishment on your way home from work—I get it! But if you're eating fast, prepared, or processed foods on a regular basis, or you're just unable to do even simple meal prep on a day off so it's easier to eat healthfully on the days that you are working, then that could be a warning flag that life may be a bit out of balance.

After eating and cleaning up, evening is the perfect time for grounding activities. You might enjoy playing an instrument or a game with a family member. Perhaps you enjoy sewing or doing puzzles. Watching television qualifies as a passive activity, but not if you're watching something violent. Inflammatory news programs can stimulate your sympathetic nervous system, working against your efforts to wind down. Simple comedies, documentaries, interviews, and biographies can be entertaining without raising your blood pressure.

Reading a book or listening to a podcast is another way to relax before bed. Just be sure to use blue light blocking lenses or settings on any electronic devices (including while watching television!) to prevent stimulating your wakefulness. Many people watch TV in bed or as a habit to fall asleep, but bed needs to be reserved exclusively for sleep and sex. Since artificial lights signal the brain to stay awake, watching television or indulging in other "screen time" activities before bed can be counterproductive.

With healthy sleep, your body experiences predictable changes:

- reduced blood pressure
- reduced heart rate
- reduced body temperature
- muscle relaxation
- slower respiratory rate

Any conditions that promote these physiological changes are conducive to good sleep: listening to calming music, taking a cool shower or ending your shower with cooler water, and lowering the temperature in your bedroom. White noise, like the sound of a fan or an air purifier, can help to mask any distracting sounds (neighbors, outside noise, even the noise in your own mind!) to promote relaxation. Practicing some gentle stretches before bed can also help to release muscle tension and support healthy sleep. Conversely, vigorous exercise too close to bedtime can raise your blood pressure, heart rate, and body temperature, as well as tighten muscles that need to relax. While some find the sound of television to be relaxing, beware of the stimulation of lights flashing and even sudden sounds.

General sleep hygiene guidelines are:

- No caffeine after noon/lunch or within 10 hours of bedtime due to the half-life and second pass effects of caffeine. Basically, a cup of coffee at noon equates to one-fourth cup at 10 p.m. Your body may be more or less sensitive, so awareness is key. Notice how your mind and body metabolize and respond to stimulants, and adjust accordingly.

- No alcohol three to four hours before bed. If you enjoy an evening cocktail and it's a safe choice for you, it's best to consume it before your evening meal.

- No food two to three hours before bed. This allows time for your body to digest properly and for blood sugar levels to stabilize so you can rest easily. As already mentioned, eating too heavily or too close to bedtime can lead to indigestion, acid reflux, weight gain, and disrupted sleep. If you must snack before bedtime, try to keep it light—some simple whole grains or a handful of nuts can provide enough substance for you to feel satisfied without essentially consuming another small meal before bed.

- No drinking one to two hours before bed. This allows time for you to empty your bladder so you're not as likely to wake up to urinate. If you're thirsty or need to take medication with water before bed, simply sip enough to quench your thirst rather than drinking a tall glass.

- No vigorous exercise two to three hours before bed. Any activity that increases your heart rate, blood pressure, respiration, muscle tone, and body temperature could interfere with your sleep. In contrast, gentle stretches may help to *decrease* heart rate, blood pressure, respiration, muscle tone, and body temperature to support healthy sleep.

- No screens/electronics one hour before bed. This can be the biggest challenge for many people! Students typically read, study notes, and write papers/do homework on tablets and computers, often late at night or shortly before bedtime. According to a 2021 survey by the Pew Research Center, 67 percent of Americans read in print, while 26 percent read e-books, with the number of electronic books and periodicals increasing steadily. That translates into a lot of screen time. To preserve your natural biorhythm and prevent overstimulation of the pineal gland and wakefulness, you can either shut off your phone notifications and devices an hour before bed, or you can use blue light blocking glasses or night settings on your screens.

Nighttime Pitta

Okay, great, you've been mindful of your eating, drinking, and activity throughout the day and you're ready for bed. Now what? From roughly 10:00 p.m. to 2:00 a.m., you cycle through pitta again. While you may recall that pitta is when your digestive fire is at its peak, this is not an invitation to get up to indulge in a midnight snack! Sleep is not just when the body slows down. In fact, there's a whole lot happening after you tuck into bed. Nighttime pitta is when your body detoxifies or literally burns away the toxins and stresses of the day. Your vital organs are busy removing wastes and impurities to cleanse and protect both your physical and mental wellness. Sleep deprivation is well known to decrease immunity—your body simply doesn't have time to tidy up and take out the trash!

Recall a time (perhaps now!) when you've felt so busy that you've neglected some of your home upkeep, when the piles of clutter have crept up and the dust bunnies have started to propagate in the corners. This happens in the home of your body as well; when you don't get adequate sleep to remove harmful chemicals and wastes, they accumulate and cause illness. Healthy digestion, detoxification, and elimination look like regular bowel movements in the morning, not constipation or diarrhea. If you're experiencing irregular elimination, it may be time to look at your daily routine, foods, and activities to see what you might tweak in order to feel better.

What about your mind? Current understanding is that ideally your mind needs to cycle through five complete sleep cycles—roughly 90 to 120 minutes each, give or take—to experience the optimum physical and mental benefits of sleep. You can think of your sleep cycle as being composed of four stages: three non-REM (N1, N2, and N3) and one REM sleep. These cycles occur roughly in order, hopefully four to five times each night.

N1 lasts about 5 to 10 percent of your typical sleep time. It's that initial light sleep from which you're easily woken. During this "la-la" stage, it's common to experience some muscle twitching (have you ever jerked yourself awake shortly after falling asleep?) before falling into deeper sleep. N2 and N3 make up about 65 to 75 percent of healthy sleep and are important for memory consolidation and learning. Since you're not likely to remember what you've read or learned in the last 10 minutes before sleep, trying to cram in information right before bed is likely to be overstimulating and unlikely to be retained. But what you've read, heard, and experienced throughout the day is consolidated, much like defragmenting a disc or computer file, so you can assimilate new learning. Non-REM sleep is largely a time to "sleep to remember."

REM sleep is a vulnerable state in nature: except for your eyes and your muscles of respiration, all of your other muscles are paralyzed. Paralysis might seem pretty dangerous from an evolutionary standpoint, so why would nature design your body to be physically at risk from predators while you slumber in REM for roughly 20 to

25 percent of the night? REM sleep clearly has an important physiological purpose in our health and long-term well-being. Otherwise, we would have become extinct or simply eaten by our nocturnal enemies while we slept.

Today it's believed that REM serves the important functions of processing trauma and desensitization of emotional experiences. When you recall a stressful event from the day, such as a near-collision while driving, your brain doesn't know the difference between imagining it in your mind versus experiencing it in real life. Living through a traumatic event, such as a terrorist act or a violent storm, causes your blood pressure to rise, your heart rate to increase, your body temperature to elevate (think perspiration!), and your skeletal muscles to contract in preparation for the fight-or-flight response. Blood flow drains away from your organs of digestion and elimination. Similarly, just imagining or recalling a traumatic or stressful event (like watching media coverage of violence over and over again) causes these same physiological responses in your body. Your brain simply can't tell the difference between real and imagined, which is why mindfulness and monitoring of your thoughts and self-talk are so critical!

Circling back to how this plays out in your sleep, REM is an opportunity to recall a stressful or traumatic event *without experiencing the sympathetic response* because your skeletal muscles are paralyzed. In this way, you can process and desensitize the experience by repeating it without the sympathetic stress reaction. Over time and with repetition, this attenuates the memory of the event so you become more of a casual observer than a victim. REM allows for emotional health by gradually peeling away the layers of emotional and physical reactivity and allowing for the distance of perspective and witness. In this way, REM is how you "sleep to forget."

With this understanding, you can appreciate how sleep deprivation and sleep disruption (think apnea and insomnia) cause and exacerbate mental disease: depression, anxiety, attention deficit, brain fog/memory loss, and impaired focus. In contrast to the concept of post-traumatic stress disorder (PTSD) being an event(s) that happened in the past, persistent traumatic stress disorder describes stressful events that continue to occur in reality or in your mind because the events have not been processed and attenuated in order to heal. When you're not able to relieve the anxiety of daily stress or persistent trauma during your sleeping life, you can become overly anxious during your waking life. Excessive anxiety can interfere with the ability to focus, and can short-circuit your ability to learn new information, recall events, and remember conversations. Brain fog and memory loss contribute to feelings of inadequacy and low self-esteem, which perpetuate overwhelm and depression. And so the vicious cycle goes—all in the name of inadequate sleep! Our beings were not designed to sleep roughly one-third of our entire existence for no reason whatsoever. Quality sleep is critical!

But what if you are a night owl who goes to bed much later than 10:00 p.m.? What's the harm there? The answer: it depends. You may function just fine, or at least think that you do, with a delayed circadian rhythm, meaning you go to bed late and you get up later. But if you find that you wake up feeling groggy, "puffy," or stiff, perhaps it's not working very well. Have you ever had the experience that you're dozing off, maybe in front of the television or while reading before bed, but for whatever reason you push through it and stay up another hour or two, only to find that you've caught a "second wind"? This may work well if you're trying to stay up late to study or to work the third shift, but if your goal is to get a good night's sleep, it's best to go to bed before you become wakeful again.

If this is something that you're struggling with, even from time to time, there are a few strategies you can employ. First, if you have a habitually delayed circadian rhythm where everything is shifted later, 0.5 to 1 mg of melatonin three hours before your desired bedtime may help to reset your clock. This is not a sedative-hypnotic dose, nor is it a sleeping pill. Combined with the sleep hygiene that we've already discussed (winding down, low lights, muscle relaxation, cool temperature, etc.) and an awareness of how your choices throughout the day impact your sleep quality at night (when and what you eat and drink, when and how you exercise, etc.), temporarily using low-dose melatonin can be safe and useful for most individuals. As with any medication or supplement, it's best to consult your medical provider regarding your individual situation.

Second, when you find yourself awake, especially when it's more frequently than once in a while, you can use cognitive behavioral therapy for insomnia. Basically, when you catch yourself becoming stressed or irritated about being wakeful when you want to sleep, listen to your self-talk. Are you catastrophizing, awful-izing, and horrible-izing? Do you tell yourself that you're never going to fall asleep, that you're going to be exhausted and nonfunctional in the morning, that you feel miserable and your mind won't quiet down long enough for you to fall asleep? Rather than toss and turn restlessly for longer than 20 to 30 minutes, remember that you should get up out of bed while keeping the lights low and read or do something quietly, like folding laundry, until you feel sleepy enough to resume sleep again.

What you don't want to do is associate bed and sleep with stress and performance anxiety. If bed is becoming stressful, you may benefit from changing your story about it. You can turn the negative thoughts around:

- "I'll never fall asleep" becomes "I will fall asleep when I relax and I'm ready."
- "I'll be exhausted all day and won't be able to function" becomes "I will manage just fine during the day, even if I feel a bit sleepy, and I can take a nap or rest my eyes for even a minute to restore myself."
- "My mind won't stop and I feel miserable!" becomes "As I release tension from my muscles and slow my breathing mindfully, my mind settles and I feel more peaceful."

In a nutshell, being in tune with the rhythms of your body, the day, and the season of the year helps you to align with your optimum health.

■ ■ ■

Diet

To be clear, when I use the word "diet" I am referring to "the kinds of foods that an individual habitually eats." We can extend this to include any solids, liquids, and substances that an individual consumes, including supplements, smoking, or consuming other nonfood items. We'll be talking about diet in terms of nutrition, and food as potent medicine that can be used as a tool to both promote wellness and heal imbalances.

Nutrition

Making time for healthy nutrition can be challenging in the face of all of life's busy-ness. When you're working 12-plus hour shifts and barely have time to let your head hit the pillow before having to be up and awake to do it all over again, there's not a lot of time or energy left over to plan, shop, or prepare nutritious meals, let alone enjoy eating them! But there are big payoffs for paying attention to how you're fueling your body. In traditional wisdom like āyurveda, food is considered to be like medicine: there are ways to practice both preventive and corrective health care by paying attention to what you eat. This section is aimed at offering some simple solutions that are easy to incorporate into everyday life.

> Regardless of what your past or present habits may be, you can always begin again with the next meal, making it support and sustain you.

If you're already doing your own organic farming and making three fresh meals from scratch every day, then give yourself a pat on the back! And if the back seat of your car is littered with drive-through fast-food wrappers, empty coffee cups, bottles, and cans of soda and energy drinks, then you definitely have room for improvement.

Regardless of what your past or present habits may be, you can always begin again with the next meal, making it support and sustain you. You may be relieved to hear that I'm not about to shove any particular regimen down your throat. You don't have to observe veganism in order to be healthy. You don't have to starve yourself in order to achieve or maintain a healthy weight. What you can do is increase your awareness of what, when, and how you eat in order to understand your tendencies, as well as what's working and what's not working, then make subtle, sustainable tweaks over time. As with everything else in Elemental-Wellness, the best diet is the one that's right for you.

Generally speaking, when it comes to nutrition, remember the acronym FLOSS. As much as possible, try to eat fresh, local, organic, seasonal, and sustainable foods. While food prep and eating leftovers can save time and money, as well as conserve resources, eating food that's been sitting in the refrigerator more than three to five days is not a healthy habit. Besides the more obvious risks of microbial overgrowth and spoilage, which can ultimately make you sick, old food is just that—it's old and stale. Traditional wisdom believes that the life force energy (prana in āyurveda, qi or chi in Chinese medicine) of food diminishes over time.

My guess is that you've probably experienced that firsthand: it's the difference between eating fresh-caught fish versus fish that's been sitting in a refrigerator for a few days—you can see, smell, and taste the difference! If you've had the pleasure of picking and eating berries fresh from the bush, you know that they're sweeter and more delicious than the ones that are flown into the grocery store from half-way across the world. Those berries have been sitting for days before you take them home, then maybe another week before you consume them. They just don't have the same nutritional or energetic value.

In addition to what we eat, drink, and consume through our mouths, there is also what we ingest through the skin, which is your largest organ system! As much as 60 percent of what you apply to your skin is absorbed into your bloodstream. Therein lies the conundrum of many commercial sunscreen products. Since we've learned the dangers of sunlight radiation to skin health, the average American consumes over $15,000 in sunscreen and skincare products over their lifetime, according to a recent US Census survey.

But not all creams and lotions are created equal! Some contain ingredients that themselves can be harmful and even carcinogenic when absorbed through the skin. Unfortunately, that leaves mainly sunscreens that are zinc based, which can give you the lovely "Casper the Friendly Ghost" look, but alas, you're saving your skin. Regarding moisturizers, water-based moisturizers simply don't work, especially the ones that are chemical-laden. On the other hand, massaging your skin with natural organic oils like sesame, coconut, shea butter, and cocoa butter give your skin a natural emollience. In general, if you can't eat it, you might want to think twice about putting it on your skin or any other body part.

Expanding the term "diet" further, consider the phrase "food for thought." It's true—what you feed your mind is as important to your mental health and well-being as what you feed your physical body. If you binge on a steady diet of soap operas or social media posts (other people's drama, excess vāta), depressing news coverage (excess kapha), or violent movies or musical lyrics (excess pitta), you're not promoting your ideal health, function, and wellness.

Consider the dental office. According to an article on the National Institutes of Health's National Library of Medicine website, listening to fast music increases heart rate, systolic, and diastolic blood pressure, and listening to slow music decreases heart rate, systolic, and diastolic blood pressure.[5] This is why we mostly play "relaxing dental office music" in the office—instrumentals and light pop/coffeehouse-style music with a slower tempo and lower tones that promotes grounding and relaxation in an environment where many people feel a bit anxious.

In summary, what you take in through *all* the senses—*sound, touch, sight, taste, and smell*—matters!

Points to Ponder

The following prompts are designed to heighten your awareness of your current routines, identify what supports your wellness, and note areas where some slight tweaks might serve you better.

1. I usually go to bed at _____ and it takes me _____ minutes to fall asleep. (Ideally, if in sync with nature: around 10:00 p.m. and less than 20 minutes.)
2. I remember waking up _____ times each night. When I do wake up, I typically fall back to sleep within _____ minutes. (In sync: zero to one, and 20 minutes.)
3. I typically sleep for _____ hours per night and wake up at _____ feeling _____. (In sync: six and a half to eight hours, waking between 5:30 a.m. and 7:30 a.m., and feeling refreshed.)
4. I typically have _____ bowel movements per day that are _____ in consistency. (In sync: one that is fairly formed and solid.)
5. I drink _____ caffeinated drinks per day. The latest I consume caffeine is _____. (In sync: zero to two drinks, and 2:00 p.m., but this is also highly individualized.)
6. My typical exercise on a daily/weekly basis consists of _____. (In sync: exercise that is considered aerobic, that raises the heart rate for at least 30 minutes three to five times per week, also some stretching at the beginning and end of the day and strengthening preferably in the morning.)
7. I accomplish my main work in the _____ (morning/afternoon/evening/night). (In sync: mainly morning, and also somewhat in the afternoon.)

---

[5]   "The Effect of Classical Music on Heart Rate, Blood Pressure, and Mood" by Cyrus Darki, Jennifer Riley, Dina P. Dadabhoy, Amir Darki, and Jennifer Garetto, July 2022.

8. I drink _____ alcoholic drinks per day. The latest I typically consume alcohol is _____. (In sync: zero to one drink for women, zero to two for men, and 7:00 p.m.)

9. I eat _____ meals per day. My final meal is finished by or before _____. (In sync: three meals before 7:00 p.m.)

10. _____ percent of my meals are made from fresh, local, organic, seasonal, and sustainable foods. (In sync: up to 80 percent whenever possible, although this can fluctuate.)

11. I drink _____ glasses of water per day. I stop drinking (other than sips to quench thirst or take medicine) by or before _____. (In sync: at least four to eight glasses [32 to 64 ounces or one to two liters] before 9:00 p.m.)

12. I turn off screens and electronics, including television and my phone, or I wear blue blocking glasses after _____. (In sync: ~9:00 p.m.)

Reviewing your reflections, in what areas are you feeling that your current habits are working well for you? Where might you benefit from a shift in your routine? What one small change could you implement today to help yourself feel healthier and more energetic? _____

Commit to trying one small change at a time for up to three weeks,
and evaluate how it works for you!

8

"E" IS FOR EXERCISES

SCAN ME

The following yoga classes are intended to be available to individuals of different abilities. You can follow the link to the recorded versions, and you can use the still photos to work on individual/particular postures, or simply practice the classes without the videos. You don't have to "do" all the poses in any class! You can also mix and match to make your own practice. Some individuals thrive on the same sequence repeated over and over again, enjoying the rhythm of routine and how to experience the same practice in different ways. Others, like myself, prefer the challenge of varied practices, depending on what's most needed at the moment. There's no pressure to practice in any particular way. If you'd like to work on one posture or mini-sequence at a time, feel free to do so!

Additionally, as Swami Kripalu says, "The highest form of practice is self-awareness without judgment." When practicing yoga, that means listening to your mind and body and making choices that honor and support you. In many of the postures, I offer options to either modify a pose to make it more accessible (sitting in a chair, leaning against a tree or wall for support, using a strap/block to reach further) or variations to challenge yourself (arm balances, deeper expressions of a posture, extended holding of a posture). I can assure you that *no one* gets a prize for hurting themselves! When there is a choice, listen to your inner wisdom and choose what's best for you in the moment. What feels right one day may be different on another day depending on many factors, like the quality of your sleep, your nutrition and hydration, other activities, and psychological and emotional stressors.

> "The highest form of practice is self-awareness without judgment."

Practicing yoga, breathing, and meditation in a group, or "sangha," can embody a powerful and special energy that isn't experienced by practicing alone. And while I do enjoy taking group yoga classes with other instructors now and then, I simply don't have time to drive 20 minutes to and from a 75-minute yoga class on a regular basis—it feels like I'm losing an entire morning or evening in the process!

From that perspective, each of the following classes can be practiced at any time of day, just about anyplace (your bedroom, basement, hotel, airport, backyard, office space, breakroom—wherever!) for as short or long as you like. By staying in each pose/posture for just three breath cycles (breathing in and breathing out, preferably five-second inhalations and five-second exhalations, or whatever feels comfortable for you), you can practice an entire yoga class in 20 to 40 minutes. If you only have limited time, you might focus on a particular need that calls your attention.

On the other hand, if you have more time and you'd like to sustain a posture anywhere from 5 to 10 breath cycles, you can lengthen each class. Another option is to pick one or a few postures at a time to explore. Some days I have 10 minutes or less, so I warm up the main joints (neck, shoulders, spine, wrists, hips, and ankles) and stretch my limbs. Beyond practicing alone, you can share these exercises with others. Essentially and *elementally* there are endless options, and you get to choose as you wish!

Regarding props like blocks, straps, and blankets, I used to think that I was fairly flexible and didn't need to use any props. What I learned was that exploring and playing with props allowed me to experience yoga postures in different ways, and supported me for better alignment. It's amazing what one discovers with an open mind! In that respect, before practicing each class, you might want to gather a nonslip yoga mat, two foam yoga blocks (or you can substitute "mega" rolls of toilet paper/paper towels or a stack of books), a blanket for warmth or to cushion your knees, and a strap (or belt, dish/tea towel, or hand towel) to act as a "limb extender." Many postures can be modified or practiced while sitting in a sturdy chair. While suggestions are provided, ultimately *you know yourself best and **you are responsible for your own well-being**!* If you are working with an injury, limitation, or challenge, please consult your health care provider for advice on how to exercise and practice safely.

In particular, the Pitta Pacifying Yoga (Tending Your Inner Fire) section in this chapter can be helpful, especially if you're feeling stressed, overwhelmed, or trending toward burnout. This class is designed to temper your Fire so that it burns at a steady, sustainable glow. You can access the virtual recording via the link, and use the photos and captions to practice at your own pace, anytime, anyplace.

Check in with yourself by asking, *"What do I need right now?"* Do you need to release excess/static energy and center yourself? Try the first five photos for opening and centering. Are you feeling warm and restless? Jump into the cooling effects of Dancing Warrior. Do you only have one or two minutes in the middle of your work day in order to reset? Practice Empty Coat Sleeves wherever you are! Is your mind overheating, are you experiencing "decision fatigue," or are you having difficulty focusing? Give yourself two or more minutes for alternate nostril breathing.

On days when you're having a hard time getting out of bed/off the couch or your energy is lagging, kapha counter-balancing yoga can be helpful to get the heart pumping, the blood circulating, and the breath flowing! Again, ask yourself, *"What do I need right now?"* Did you wake up feeling unrefreshed, needing to wake yourself gently? Opening and centering may perk you up as much as a cup of coffee. Do you find yourself weighted down during the day? Perhaps the chair squat "flying" variation can help you shed that heavy feeling. Are you in need of an instant energy pick-me-up? Practice pulling prana (with or without Moon Salutation and/or Funky Monkey). Would you like to increase circulation without revving your heart rate? Maybe Supine Hand to Big Toe Pose is just what the doctor ordered. Even one or a few of the movement postures may energize you!

"What do I need right now?"

At the end of the day, or truly anytime that your mind and body are having a hard time settling down, vāta validating yoga can meet you exactly where you are. *"What do I need right now?"* Do you need help transitioning from perpetual motion to rest? Seated Vinyasa flow transforms frenetic energy into mindful movement. Are you craving your pillow? Restorative postures like Resting Pigeon, Forward Fold (Paschimottanasana), and Straddle with Forward Fold/block modification can be practiced for just a few breath cycles each, or as much as 3 to 10 minutes, as in a restorative or yin style of yoga. Having a hard time settling down toward the end of the day? Legs Up the Wall (with or without self-massage) and Three-Part/Complete Yogic Breath can be practiced before bathing/showering, on your living room floor or sofa, or in the comfort of your own bed! By dialing down the volume and velocity, this class helps to settle and ground your energy for rest and restoration.

"What do I need right now?"

Pitta Pacifying Yoga (Tending Your Inner Fire)

Find a comfortable seat, either on a cushion/block or in a chair, ideally with your hips higher than your knees. With palms together at chest height, breathe in and draw your arms overhead in Seated Mountain Pose (Tadasana).

As you breathe out, separate your fingers as if you were sprinkling confetti, releasing any cares, worries, insomnia, or anxiety. Say to yourself: "Tomorrow is a mystery." (Consider reciting to yourself all the quoted affirmations that follow.) Inhale your arms back overhead in Seated Mountain Pose and exhale down the centerline, cupping your hands over your eyes. "Present moment, perfect moment."

With the next inhalation, draw your arms up in Seated Mountain. As you exhale, cup your hands and give a "royal wave," releasing "coulda, shoulda, woulda" regret and disappointment, attachment, and depression. "Yesterday is history." Inhale your arms overhead, and exhale down the centerline, cradling your face in your hands. "You are perfect in this and every moment."

Inhale arms overhead to Mountain, and exhale as you shake off any irritation, frustration, inflammation, impatience, control, negativity, judgment, excuses, or perfectionism. "Everything is perfect in this moment."

Inhale, arms overhead, crossing at the wrists and linking your thumbs. Exhale your hands like butterfly wings that land on your collar bones in Garuda Mudra, a gesture of balancing rest and activity.

Soften and lower your gaze or close your eyes for centering. Scan your physical body for warmth/inflammation, noticing any sensations, as well as your mind-body and any judgments/criticism. Practicing presence and caring with yourself enables you to be present and caring for others. Consider the affirmation: "I embody peace and ease in the present moment."

Bringing your awareness back to the space around you, let your eyes lift/open again. Begin to trace a smile with your chin, inhaling your right ear toward your right shoulder (or lifting your left ear toward the sky), exhaling your chin toward your chest, and then inhaling your left ear toward your left shoulder (or lifting your right ear toward the sky). Continue to breathe this way, alternating sides, tracing a smile with your chin.

Placing the right palm on the ground or a block, reach the left arm overhead and to the side, feeling space between your fingers, ribs, and armpit. As you breathe in, let the breath lift your torso slightly as you smile at the sky. As you breathe out, gently reach a bit further to the side, softly undulating like gentle waves. Repeat Seated Side Stretch for a few or several breath cycles.

Come up onto your right knee (cushioning it on a blanket or pad if that supports you), and extend your left leg to the side, coming into Half Circle (Ardha Mandalasana). With each inhalation, open the fingers like a shining star, and with each exhalation, close the fingers into a loose fist as the "star" blinks out. Take three to five breath cycles.

With your next exhalation, sweep your left arm down and back behind you as you lower your buttocks to the ground, tuck your left foot behind you, and fold both knees, coming into Stag's Leap. Inhale the left arm behind you and then exhale your left arm in front of you and across the horizon to the right, clearing away any "smoke" or "fog" or anything that you don't need around you. This can be a beautiful gesture of releasing physical and mental clutter. Repeat three to five times.

Bring the left leg forward, wrapping your strap around your foot to extend your reach **OR** cradle your left knee in your left hand or elbow, holding your left foot in your right hand/elbow to open up your hip. Gaze lovingly at your knee as if it were a precious kitten/puppy/baby, and blow it a kiss! Rock your knee side to side for three to five breath cycles. Allow gratitude for your feet and legs to soften your heart.

Using a strap or belt to lengthen your limbs, extend your left leg as you flex your foot to stretch your calf and hamstring in Heron Pose (Krounchasana). Inhale, pressing your heel away; exhale and draw your toes toward your nose. Keep your knee soft and slightly bent to avoid hyperextension. After a few breaths, slide your hands down your calf/thigh for support and trace circles with your big toe, rotating your ankle 8 to 10 times in each direction. If you notice any cracks or snaps, see how smooth you can make your circles.

Bend your extended leg and cross it over your right knee, stacking your knees like firewood in Cow Face Pose (Gomukhasana)—see how the knees resemble a cow's face and the feet are its ears? Keeping the strap in your right hand, inhale and sweep your right arm overhead as you bend your elbow and pat yourself on the back—*you're doing great!* Bring the opposite arm to catch your right elbow, airing out your armpits, allowing space into your heart. *Stay here* **OR**, with the next breath, bend your left elbow and reach for the strap behind you (or release the strap if your hands naturally touch). With your hands "joined," lift your right elbow toward the sky as you inhale, and pull the left elbow down toward the earth as you exhale in a little yin-yang shoulder opener.

Release the strap if you're using it and allow both arms to float down by your sides. Bring your left foot to stand so your knee is in front of your chest. Inhale your right arm to the side and exhale as you bring your right hand toward your left hip, coming into a Twist (Matsyendrasana) like smoke spiraling up from your Fire. As you ground through your sit bones, lengthen your spine by reaching the crown of your head toward the sky, gazing over your left shoulder if that's available. With each inhalation, find a bit more space between your vertebrae, and with each exhalation twist a bit more until you reach your intelligent edge (stretching and not harming).

Unwind from your head, neck, shoulders, and spine, switch the cross of your legs and, beginning with Seated Side Stretch, repeat this sequence on the opposite side.

After repeating the sequence on the second side, make your way to hands and knees

with hips aligned over your knees and hands beneath your shoulders in Table Pose. You may find it more comfortable to use a blanket to cushion your knees. Remember the options of resting on fists **OR** hands on blocks **OR** forearms on blocks.

From table pose, raise your right hip 90 degrees into "Fire Hydrant" Pose. It's okay to smile and have fun! Begin to trace circles with your knee caps, releasing any tension/ cracks/crunches from the hip joints. Hips are considered to harbor many "campfire stories," many of which are untrue and unsupportive. Cool, loosen, and lubricate your hip as you circle your knees 8 to 10 times in both directions. Inhale, extending your right leg long behind you, and exhale your right foot to stand between your hands in Knee Down Lunge.

From Knee Down Lunge, curl the left toes under as you lift the left knee, finding yourself in High Lunge (Anjaneyasana) with both arms extended at the horizon in front of you. With both hands, trace a figure eight 8 to 10 times.

Gliding the left hand across your chest and opening to the left, pivot your left foot about 45 degrees to the long edge of your mat, finding yourself in Warrior Two

Pose (Virabhadrasana 2). In Warrior Two Pose, inhale as you extend both arms, as if you're being pulled in opposite directions. Exhale and draw the shoulder blades toward each other. Stay here for three to five breath cycles. Breathe in and envision length from your right middle finger, along your arm, and across your back to your left middle finger. Breathe out and pull the "wing tips" of your shoulders toward your core. You've got this!

From Warrior Two Pose, inhale as you flip your right palm up, then exhale as your left arm slides down your left leg in Reverse Warrior Pose. With the next inhalation, sweep the right arm forward, bringing the right elbow/forearm to the right thigh, and exhale as your left arm reaches forward in Extended Angle Pose. Continue to glide forward and back between the two postures, visualizing painting a rainbow overhead with your fingers, in Dancing Warrior. Smile!

After several breath cycles and rounds of Dancing Warrior, bring both hands to the floor/blocks and step the right foot back to meet the left foot as your hips rise toward the sky. Let your head hang like a ripe fruit, finding yourself in Downward Facing Dog Pose. "Pedal" your feet, alternately pressing one heel and then the other toward the earth, as you Walk Your Dog.

**Lower both knees to the mat in Table Pose and repeat the sequence from Fire Hydrant through Downward Facing Dog on the opposite side. When your "dog walk" is complete, slightly bend both knees and either step or hop to the front of the mat, coming to stand in Standing Mountain Pose. Pause: breathe, feel, and notice anything that has shifted.

Making your way to one-legged balancing postures, consider using a wall or sturdy object to support you as you cultivate your practice. Inhale and shift your weight to your left leg; as you exhale, bend the right knee behind you and catch it with your right hand/strap in Heel to Buttocks Pose. Option to *stay here* **OR** raise your left arm overhead as you pivot at the hips and press the right foot back firmly into the right hand, coming into Dancer Pose (Natarajasana). Option to *stay here* **OR** sweep the left hand back to join the right hand in Standing Bow Pose. Whichever option you've chosen, "exhale tension and inhale ease, exhale stress and inhale flow, exhale irritation and inhale acceptance, exhale burnout and inhale bliss." Breathe in as you release the posture and return to Standing Mountain. Pause and notice how one side may feel different from the other before repeating balance on the opposite side.

Stepping your feet to the edges of your mat, begin to swing your arms side to side, allowing your heels to stay on the mat or alternately lift, in Empty Coat Sleeves Posture. Feel the cool breeze of your arms moving through space, allowing your body to move organically for 10 or more breaths before eventually coming to natural rest. Pause in Standing Mountain Pose: breathe, release, feel, observe, and allow whatever sensations arise to be exactly as they are without judging or adjusting yourself. If you feel at all lightheaded, stand or sit in stillness, enabling yourself to settle.

Stepping your feet a few feet apart, begin to fold forward from your waist, hands sliding down your thighs and landing on your legs, a block, or the floor in front of you. **If inversion causes dizziness or discomfort, honor yourself and sit in a chair or simply bend your knees into a gentle squat with your head in whatever position most supports you.** If it's available, allow the weight of gravity to lengthen your neck and gently circle your head in both directions. Smooth any roughness or cracking/crepitus.

Bend your knees and walk your feet about shoulder width apart as you rest your elbows on your thighs, coming into your version of Garland Pose/Squatting (Malasana), as if sitting around a campfire. You can rest your bottom on a chair, a block, or stack of blocks, **OR** if it's available, you can press your tailbone toward the floor. Bringing the elbows to the inner knees/thighs with palms together, isometrically press the elbows against your legs while you press your legs into your elbows/upper arms. As you breathe, imagine sitting around a traditional fire while telling stories, singing, or working with family, friends, and community.

Stay in Garland Pose, **OR** if you'd like to practice arm balance, try placing your palms flat on the floor **OR** your forearms on low blocks while keeping your elbows/upper arms against your inner thighs. Being mindful not to rock onto your forehead (perhaps placing a blanket in front of you as a cushion, just in case), begin to shift your weight forward onto your arms. You can practice lifting one foot off the floor at a time, or lift both feet, coming into Crow Pose

(Bakasana). Wherever you are, breathe and invite ease to replace effort.

From Garland or Crow, place your palms flat on the mat in front of you, draw your knees into Table, and slide your torso back, coming onto your belly. Pressing your pelvic and pubic bones into the mat, exhale and lift your chest/torso, finding yourself in Cobra Pose. With each inhalation, feel your torso rise slightly, and with each exhalation, allow yourself to lower halfway toward the mat like a wave.

Stay in Cobra, undulating with your breath, **OR** return to your belly with your chin or forehead touching your mat. Place your hands alongside your thighs, palms facing down. Inhale, pressing your pubic and pelvic bones onto the mat. Exhale and lift your torso and legs, finding yourself in Locust Pose (Salabhasana). Breathe for a few or several cycles, as if floating on water or clouds, envisioning the crown of your head lifting toward Space, sun and stars, and your hips supported by the stability of Earth.

With the next exhalation, lower yourself to the mat, place your palms near your shoulders, and press your hips back toward your feet, coming into Child's Pose (Balasana). Rest, breathe, feel, and allow.

From Child's Pose, press into your palms and walk your hands back through sitting, swing your legs in front of you, and make your way to lie on your back. With arms extended by your sides, palms facing down, step flexed feet on the sky in Legs Up the Wall Pose (Viparita Karani). You can *stay in this gentle inversion,* **OR** for more vigor, you can bring the feet about a leg's width apart and then cross at the ankles in Scissors. With each inhalation, release the cross, and with each exhalation, cross again at the ankles, alternating which foot is forward, strengthening your core and inner thighs.

Continue Scissors for as long as it feels right for you. Imagine hearing birds singing, feeling the sun shining on your face, gazing at blue skies, tasting fresh air, and smelling the scent of green leaves.

When your inversion is complete, bend both knees and hug them toward your chest or armpits in Apanasana. Rock yourself side to side or massage your low back by rolling in small circles. Prepare for relaxation by wearing socks or a

sweater/blanket if you tend to become cool, and otherwise make yourself comfortable lying flat on your mat in Savasana. (If your low back is tender, bend your knees with feet flat on the edges of your mat and tip your knees to touch.) Rest and breathe naturally to integrate, closing your eyes if it's comfortable. Take five minutes or longer for deep relaxation.

As you are ready and relaxation feels complete, invite gentle movement into your fingers and toes. Roll onto one side and pause before pressing yourself up to sit. Bring your right thumb to close your right nostril and inhale up the left side. Close the left nostril with your right ring finger, release your thumb and exhale out the right side. Inhale up the right, close the right nostril with your thumb and open the left as you exhale. Continue alternating sides in Alternate Nostril Breathing (Nadi Shodhana). When you feel complete, make your final exhalation out the left side, release, and return to your natural breath. Notice what, if anything, has shifted.

Where the mind goes, energy flows.

Namaste

Kapha Counter-Balance
(Energy Enhancing)

Find a comfortable seat, either on a cushion/block or in a chair, ideally with your hips higher than your knees. With palms together at chest height, breathe in and draw your arms overhead in Seated Mountain Pose (Tadasana).

As you exhale, extend your arms, separating your fingers like the rays of the sunrise, radiating out. As you inhale into Mountain Pose again, imagine the shoots of a flower rising in springtime; exhale, extend your arms, and separate your fingers, envisioning the flower petals blooming. Inhale once more and lift your gaze toward the sky like a baby bird lifting its beak; exhale and let your baby bird spread its wings and fly out of the nest, feeling independence and the space all around you.

Beautiful.

Bring your thumb and middle finger pads to touch, and let the backs of your hands rest on your lap in Akasha Mudra, the gesture of Space with the qualities of Vastness and Possibility. Soften and lower your gaze or close your eyes for centering. Feel the Earth-like weight of your muscles, soft and dense, and your bones, smooth and solid. Now notice the light and subtle qualities of a single eyelash. Notice any areas of congestion or phlegm, and then bring your awareness to the space and clarity of your ear canal. Draw your attention to your thoughts and mind-body, and notice if anything feels "stuck" or heavy. Is there any part of you that's curious about what this practice will encompass? Know that as you practice self-awareness and self-care, you bring your best self to the world. Consider the affirmation: *"I am infinite."*

Bring your awareness back to the space around you. Begin with Kapalabhati (Skull Polishing) Breath to clear congestion from the sinuses/chest and "cobwebs" from the mind. **Note: If you are pregnant, menstruating, have IBS or had recent abdominal surgery, practice very gently.** As if blowing out a single candle with your nose, inhale halfway through your nose and exhale crisply out your nose, feeling your belly contract on its own. Repeat this rhythmically for 10 to 20 breath cycles, exhaling crisply and allowing the inbreath to happen automatically. Pause and clear any coughing/mucus. Repeat for another 20 to 40 breath cycles. Pause and

notice if the practice has ignited your Fire or burned off any cloudiness/congestion. Maybe it has, maybe it hasn't. Just notice without judgment.

If you've been seated on any prop, remove and set it aside. Placing your palms on your kneecaps, inhale and arch forward, lifting your chest, chin, and gaze as your tailbone lifts, finding yourself in Seated Cow Pose (Bitilasana).

Exhale and round your back, gaze coming toward your belly or groin, finding yourself in Seated Cat Pose (Marjaryasana). Continue to flow between Seated Cow Pose and Seated Cat Pose, inhaling forward and exhaling back, beginning to wake up the shoulders, the back, the spine, and the hips.

As you inhale forward, begin to turn and churn toward one side, exhaling all the way back into Seated Cat Pose, and then inhaling up the opposite side as you return to Seated Cow Pose. Continue to exhale down and around, and inhale up and forward. See how much energy and movement you can invite into the side ribs and neck. After five revolutions in one direction, pause in the center and continue for five revolutions in the opposite direction. In the morning, this is the "Coffee Grinder"—wake up and smell the coffee! At other times, this is your "Pepper Mill"—go ahead and spice things up! Add some flavor to savor!

With bent knees, place your feet about mat-width apart in front of you, and place your hands on the floor, palms facing down behind you with fingertips facing away. Inhale, and as you exhale, let both knees drop to one side. Inhale the knees back to center, and exhale as knees drop to the other side.

As you continue to breathe and twist, you can leave your hands behind you for support **OR** allow your arms to reach around/behind you for a greater twist. Continue to alternate knee drops/twists to each side for 5 to 10 breath cycles.

The next time you find yourself off to one side, come up onto one knee, support yourself with the same side hand/arm, and sweep the opposite arm overhead and behind you, coming into Half Circle (Ardha Mandalasana). Breathe in and breathe out. As you hold the pose, begin to trace some figure eights with your top hand to open up your shoulder. Draw five figure eights in one direction, and then draw five in the opposite direction, seeing how much space you can glide through. Let your extended arm come down, your hips kiss the floor. Make your way off to Half Circle and draw figure eights on the other side. Imagine the sun shining warmly on your face.

Let your hips come back to the mat and briefly roll onto hands and knees in Table Pose. Curl the toes under so the tips of your big toes touch the mat.

Lift the hips toward the sky as you straighten your legs, and find yourself in Downward Facing Dog (Adho Mukkha Svanasana). Stay here, allowing the weight of your head to hang like a ripe melon, **OR** begin to alternately bend one knee as you straighten the other, pedaling your feet as you "walk your dog."

From Downward Facing Dog, bend both knees and allow your heels to lift further away from the mat. Options are to step one foot and then the other forward to the front of your mat **OR** hop both feet forward to the front of your mat. Roll all the way up to standing and roll your shoulders back, making your way into Mountain Pose (Tadasana), and breathe naturally. Notice if anything has shifted energetically. Perhaps you feel more alive, awake, blood circulating, "ready to go." You're doing great already!

Inhale hands to hips, and exhale as you step your left foot back into High Lunge. If you feel

unsteady, you can step your feet further toward the edges of your mat. Inhale and draw both arms out to the horizon in front of you, palms together. Begin to trace figure eights with your hands for 10 revolutions, waking up the wrists, elbows, and shoulders.

From High Lunge, inhale and draw both arms overhead as you straighten both knees. As you exhale, let both arms float down by your sides (like your baby bird is flying out of the nest!) as your front knee bends into High Lunge again. Continue to flow, inhaling arms overhead as knees straighten, exhaling your "wings" through the air as your front knee bends. Flow for five or more breath cycles, feeling your "bird" gather confidence and momentum as you fly through the blue sky.

The next time you inhale your arms overhead, bend your front knee, exhale into a High Lunge, and bend your elbows like "goal posts." Lift your gaze toward the sky and arch your back slightly as you draw your elbows back like a proud pigeon or a robin with the sun shining down upon its chest. Hold the posture and breathe for at least three complete breath cycles. Inhale again, then bring both hands to the front thigh. Step the back foot forward to meet the front foot, returning to Mountain Pose. Pause and notice whether one leg feels different from the other.

Inhaling in Mountain Pose, exhale as you step the right foot back into High Lunge and repeat this sequence on the right side. When you find yourself in High Lunge with "goal posts," consider the option of bringing both arms behind you and clasping your hands for an even greater heart opener. Be mindful that most of us have habitual ways of doing things, and practicing on opposite sides/directions can be helpful to break up stickiness/stagnation while inviting creativity and energy. Variety is the spice of life!

Inhale again, then bring both hands to the front thigh. Step the back foot forward to meet the front foot, returning to Mountain Pose. Breathe in, hands to hips, and breathe out into Chair Squat (Utkatasana). Breathing in, bring the arms up overhead; breathing out, sweep both arms to one side and behind you. Continue to flow side to side, inhaling arms up and exhaling arms behind you as you "clear clutter." Move slowly and gracefully **OR** with more vigor, feeling free and light, soaring, flying, and gliding. Let yourself naturally come to stillness in Mountain Pose. Pause and notice the effects on your heartbeat and breath.

After pausing in Mountain Pose for a minute, begin the following sequence, Moon Salutation (Chandra Namaskar):

Inhale and sweep both arms up overhead, palms together. Exhale and let your hips shift to one side as the upper body leans the opposite way in Crescent/Half Moon (Ardha Chandrasana). Inhale arms overhead again as you straighten your torso into Tall Mountain Pose, and exhale into Crescent/Half Moon on the other side.

Inhale as you step one foot out to the side, exhale as you drop your seat into Goddess Pose (Deviasana).

Inhale and straighten all your limbs into Five Pointed Star as you lengthen your spine. Exhale one arm down the same side leg into a side stretch. Breathe in and rise back up into Five Pointed Star; breathe out and reach into a side stretch on the other side.

Inhale back into Five Pointed Star, exhale and cross one hand toward the opposite leg/foot into a cross-twist. *Remember, this is a direction, not a destination. Stretch to your intelligent limit/edge/challenge, NEVER to pain!* Breathe up into Five Pointed Star, breathe out as you cross-twist the opposite way. Inhale back into Five Pointed Star, exhale as you sit back down into Goddess Pose.

Inhale arms overhead, hands and feet together, in Tall Mountain Pose, exhale into Crescent Moon as you begin another one to two rounds of Moon Salutation.

OPTIONAL arm/core strengthening energizer series (Pulling Prana/Life Force Energy):

1. In Goddess Pose, inhale your arms out to goal posts and then exhale your elbows toward each other in front of your chest.

2. Inhale, reaching your arms overhead, and then exhale, pulling elbows down by your side ribs.

3. Inhale, extend both arms forward in front of you at the horizon, and then exhale as you bend your elbows and draw them alongside your ribs, curling your hands into fists. Repeat these three arm movements 10 times **OR** add High Intensity Interval Training by alternately lifting one foot/knee and then the other while Pulling Prana in what I affectionately call the "Funky Monkey"!

Whichever variation you've chosen, remember, it's okay to play, be silly, and have fun! From Goddess, to complete the Moon Salutation, inhale arms overhead, hands and feet together. Take one more Crescent Moon to both sides. In Mountain, trace a full moon with your fingertips, bring your hands to heart center, and breathe. Release, feel, and notice. Soak in the energy and resources around you; feel life force energy circulating within you. There's no right or wrong—there's only your experience.

Make your way to the top of your mat for one-legged standing balance. If you're cultivating balance, you may choose to practice next to a wall or a sturdy piece of furniture to support yourself. Inhale with your hands on your hips, and as you exhale, bend your knees and come into Chair Squat **OR** sit at the edge of a sturdy chair. Let the weight shift onto one leg, come up onto the opposite toe, and cross your lifted leg onto the standing leg in Figure 4. Stay here, practicing balance and opening the hip, **OR** raise the arm on the standing leg side up overhead and bend your elbow. **Option:** Sweep the other arm up to catch your bent elbow and draw it toward your backbone, giving yourself a pat on the back—you're doing great! Whichever option you've chosen, breathe in and lengthen your spine; breathe out and open the hip a bit more. After three to five breath cycles, unwind the arms and legs and straighten out of the squat into Mountain. Pause and notice any differences in one side versus the other. Repeat the posture on the opposite side. Oh my goodness! You've got this!

Coming to the front of your mat **OR** the edge of your chair, inhale the hands to hips so that your thumbs wrap around your back and your fingers wrap around the front of your hips. Tuck your chin toward your chest to protect your neck. Inhale, and as you exhale begin to arch your back into a slight backbend in Camel Pose (Ustrasana). Exhale stagnation, inhale the new. Exhale sadness, inhale joy. Exhale boredom, inhale excitement. Exhale *Burnout*, inhale *Bliss*! Bring yourself upright and take a few moments, especially if you feel at all lightheaded, and breathe naturally.

Inhale your arms up overhead, and as you exhale, pivot from the hips, folding forward in a swan dive. Inhale halfway up and exhale, folding a little further. Take a bend in the knees, place both hands on the mat, and make your way through Table Pose onto your belly. Extend both hands overhead flat on the mat, palms facing down. Place your forehead or chin on the mat. Inhale and lengthen; exhale as you slide your left hand by your left thigh, palm facing down. Inhale, pressing into your pelvis, your left palm, and top of your right foot. Exhale and lift your right arm, left leg, and chest in Diagonal Stretch (Salabhasana variation) **OR** option to lift only the arm or leg. There should be no pain. Lift slightly as you breathe in; lower on exhale for three to five breath cycles. Return to the starting position and repeat on the opposite side.

Exhale all the way down, bring your palms by your chest, and press up to sitting. Swing your legs long and flat in front of you. Bend the left knee and place the left insole against the right thigh. Breathe in, accessing length in your spine; breathe out and walk your hands along your right leg, coming into Forward Fold/Head to Knee Pose (Janu Sirsasana). Use your block and/ or fist to make a pillow for yourself in Thinker Pose. Hold for three to five breath cycles. As you expand your body, you expand your mind. Inhale all the way up to sitting, switch the legs, and repeat on the opposite side. Feel space under your armpit and beneath your chin and neck.

Coming to sit upright, move any blocks out of the way, and gather your strap as you make your way onto your back. Step both flexed feet onto the sky, and then loop your strap around the soles of your feet. Inhale, pressing your legs long, and as you exhale release the left leg long and flat on the mat, leaving the right leg skyward in preparation for Supine Hand-to-Big Toe Pose (Supta Padangusthasana A-B-C):

1. Inhale and press the right heel away, exhale and draw the toes toward your nose, keeping the right knee soft. Repeat for two more breath cycles.
2. Inhale and take the strap into your right hand; exhale and guide your right leg to the right in a half straddle. Breathe in, pressing the heel away, and breathe out, drawing the right toes in the direction of your right ear. Repeat for two breath cycles.
3. Inhale, guiding the right leg back overhead as in the beginning, switching the strap to the left hand. Exhale and cross the right leg over to the left side in a supine twist while keeping both shoulders grounded on the mat. Inhale, pressing the right heel away; exhale as you bring the right toes a bit closer to the left ear. Gaze can be toward the left, toward the sky, or toward the right for a greater twist. Repeat for two more breath cycles. Inhale as you return the right foot to the ceiling; exhale as you bring the left foot to meet the right. Pause and notice if it appears that one leg has gotten slightly longer than the other. With the strap looped around your soles, inhale, pressing the left foot skyward, and exhale as you release the right leg long and flat on the mat. Repeat Supine Hand-to-Big Toe Pose on the opposite side. When you have completed both sides, step both feet skyward and notice if your legs appear to be the same length.

Bend both knees and release the strap off to the side. Clasp the outer edges of your feet in Happy Baby (Ananda Balasana). Go ahead and rock, play, and explore by moving through space. Babies explore their world with curiosity, wonder, and joy!

Extend your legs long for Deep Relaxation (Savasana), or place your feet at the edges of your mat and bend your knees if your low back is tender. Take several minutes to integrate all the beautiful energy that's been accessed. Breathe naturally. After several minutes, begin to wiggle your fingers and toes, introducing some micromovements. Pull your knees toward your chest or armpits and rock off onto one side, resting briefly before bringing yourself up to sitting.

The peace of yoga,
Grounding and Energizing,
Is with you, always.

Namaste

Vāta Validating Yoga

Find yourself a comfortable seat, perhaps on a cushion or a block to elevate your hips. Inhale your arms out to the sides and overhead as you scoop up everything around you that's calling your attention. With fingertips together, exhale down the centerline—condensing, sifting, filtering. Repeat for two more breath cycles, inhaling and sweeping up, exhaling and settling down your energy.

From a loose fist, point your index and middle fingers into a "peace sign," in Bhu Mudra, the gesture of Earth with the qualities of stability and grounding. Extend your fingers down toward the earth, as if you are plugging in or rooting down, and lower your gaze/close your eyes for centering. Notice areas of your body that feel frenetic, and then feel yourself stable and supported in your seat. Bring your attention to the movement of your thoughts, and then bring your awareness back to your breath in the present moment. "Following the rhythmic flow of your breath, the mind finds a natural place of rest." Continue to breathe naturally, and see if you can lengthen the breath cycle to five seconds out and five seconds in. If that's not available, just slow to a rhythm that's comfortable for you. Slower, grounding breaths can be soothing.

Continuing with your slow or five-second breaths, inhale and extend your arms out in front of your chest, palms facing up, beginning a Seated Vinyasa Flow.

Exhale, bending the elbows, and cup your hands over your eyes.

Breathing in with palms together, draw the arms up overhead as you open the palms forward to let the backs of your hands touch in Tall Seated Mountain (Tadasana). Bring your right hand to your left wrist, and exhale to the right for a side stretch (Ardha Chandrasana). Inhale back to Tall Seated Mountain, switch the clasp of your wrists, and exhale into a side stretch on the opposite side.

Inhale to Tall Seated Mountain, exhale and turn to the right as you extend both arms out to the horizon, and then bring your left hand to your right hip, right hand behind you in a Seated Twist (Bharadvajasana). Option to take another breath cycle as you gaze over your right shoulder. With the next inhalation, raise your arms overhead, front and center in Tall Seated Mountain, exhale and turn to the left as you extend both arms out to the horizon and then bring your right hand to your left hip, left hand behind you in a Seated Twist. Option to take another breath cycle as you gaze over your left shoulder.

Inhale and unwind from the twist, arms front and center overhead in Tall Seated Mountain. Interlace the fingers and evert the palms to face skyward. Exhale and round over, gazing toward your belly button or groin in Seated Cat (Marjaryasana).

Inhale as you separate the fingers and "breaststroke" your arms to the sides, then exhale as you interlace your hands behind you, lifting your chest, chin, and gaze as your shoulders melt down your back, arching into Seated Cow (Bitilasana).

Inhale as you shrug your shoulders toward your ears, interlacing your fingers at heart center, and exhale as you press your palms toward your lap, reaching each ear alternately toward the sky, lengthening your neck.

Begin this Seated Vinyasa Flow again, starting from "inhale and extend your arms out in front of your chest, palms facing up."

Repeat the series for three rounds, or as much as feels good/you have time for.

Roll off of your prop or block, if you've been sitting on one, and make your way to hands and knees, perhaps cushioning your knees with a blanket or pillow. If your wrists are tender, you can come onto fists **OR** rest hands/forearms on foam blocks. Whichever option you've chosen, check that your wrists are under your shoulders and your knees are aligned under your hips in Table Pose.

Inhale the left knee at a 90-degree angle in "Fire Hydrant" Pose, and exhale the left knee in the *direction* of your left shoulder (it doesn't have to touch!) in a side crunch.

Inhale and reach the left leg long, crossing behind you so your left big toe reaches for/touches down on the right side as you gaze over your right shoulder in a cross-tuck.

Continue to glide back and forth between postures, lubricating the hips as you exhale to side crunch and inhale to cross-tuck for 3 to 10 repetitions, slowly, as if moving through molasses or creamy peanut butter!

The last time you inhale into cross-tuck, exhale and bring the left knee between your hands all the way down to the mat. You can support your left hip with a block or cushion under your buttocks. Lean forward and rest your forehead on a block/

hands/pillow in Resting Pigeon (Kapotasana). Breathe and stretch your hips in this restorative variation for 30 to 60 seconds.

From Resting Pigeon, inhale as you remove any props from under your hips and lift up, bringing hands to blocks in front of you, stepping your left foot between your hands in Knee-Down Lunge (Anjaneyasana).

Exhale and shift the hips back, front leg straightening into a Half-Split Pose (Ardha Hanumanasana). Keep the front knee soft to avoid hyperextension. Continue to inhale forward as you bend the front knee into Knee-Down Lunge, and exhale as your hips shift back into Ardha Hanumanasana, in a cleanse (Kriya), squeezing stale blood and toxins out of your muscles in one movement and allowing fresh blood to soak your muscles with oxygen and nutrients. Repeat for 3 to 10 breath cycles.

The next time you find yourself in Knee-Down Lunge, curl the right toes under, lift the right knee, and press up into High Lunge. Find Bhu Mudra and circle your wrists 10 times in each direction. If there are any cracks or "crunchiness" in the wrists, see how smoothly you can make circles. Vāta validation doesn't mean the absence of movement. It just means we turn down the velocity and volume a bit. Nice!

Placing both hands flat on the mat or blocks, step the left foot back to meet the right as you engage your core, finding yourself in Plank Pose (Vashistasana). Options are to bring your knees down to the mat **OR** lower down like a reverse push-up in Chaturanga, and flow back to Table Pose.

Repeat the flow from Table Pose through High Lunge on the opposite side.

Inhale, step both feet to the front of your mat, and roll up into Standing Tall Mountain (Tadasana). Pause for a minute and soak in the effects of your practice thus far.

Make your way to the front of your mat and roll your feet/ankles side to side and heel to toe, then "'suction" all the edges of your feet into the mat. Inhale, letting your weight come into the left leg as you turn your right knee out to a 90-degree angle. Slide the right instep into the left ankle in Kickstand Tree, **OR** slide the right instep up the left calf muscle, **OR** bring the right foot into the left thigh for *your* variation of Tree Pose (Vrksasana). (Avoid pressing directly against your knee!) Inhale arms overhead, palms together; exhale arms out to the sides like branches. Consider micro-movements, lifting your arms slightly with each inhalation and lowering just a bit with each exhalation, like leaves/branches in a gentle breeze.

After 3 to 10 breath cycles in Tree Pose, inhale both hands to your bent knee and exhale as you draw the knee toward your belly/chest in Wind-Relieving Pose to promote digestion. Circle your feet/ankles 10 times in each direction. Constant motion can contribute to fatigue and constipation; the antidote is to rest and digest!

Inhale and extend the right knee out at a 90-degree angle, as if you were stepping on a rock in Crane Pose. You can imagine your arms extended in Bhu Mudra like cables connecting you to the earth, grounding down, steady. Inhale and set both feet down, allow the arms to rest by your sides, and breathe for 30 to 60 seconds. Notice how one side might feel different from the other.

Repeat Tree through Crane on other side.

After practicing one-legged standing balance on the right and left legs, pause 30 to 60 seconds and notice what may have settled or shifted for you.

Stand at the top of your mat, feet hip-width apart. Inhale arms up overhead, exhale forward, folding at the hips. Inhale halfway up and exhale, folding a bit further. Lift and lower for one more breath, keeping your knees soft, and then bend both knees. Bring your hands down to the mat and come all the way down onto your belly.

Bring your elbows beneath your shoulders, coming into Sphinx Pose. Feel your hand and forearms grounding down as if glued to the mat. Inhale, pressing your pelvis into the mat, and exhale lifting your chest and torso. Imagine that you are a sphinx, solid as a statue at the entrance of a museum, steady no matter how much commotion surrounds. After 3 to 10 breaths, inhale and walk the hands back toward your hips as you press up to sit.

Swing both legs around in front of you, coming to sit on your bottom. You might want to have blocks handy. Inhale, lengthening your spine. As you exhale, begin to walk your hands forward as you fold at the hips. Inhale, rising up, and exhale, folding a bit deeper for two more breath cycles. On your third exhalation, make a support with one or more blocks/fists and rest your head in Forward Fold (Paschimottanasana). Feel

the support of the earth as you rest for 30 to 60 seconds.

Begin to lift up from the forward fold and come into a Straddle (Upavistha Konasana) with your blocks in front of you. Exhale as you walk your hands forward; inhale as you walk your hands back up to sitting. See how much you can release with each breath. You can rest your head again on the block(s) for 30 to 60 seconds. Forward

folds can be soothing to the central nervous system.

Begin to walk your hands back up to sitting and swing your legs together in front of you as you come to lie on your back. Inhale, bending both knees as you step your feet on the mat, and then cross your right leg over the left

as if sitting cross-legged in a chair. Breathing in, press your palms and feet into the mat, lift your hips just an inch and to the right just an inch, then exhale as you set your hips down on the mat. Let both knees roll over toward the left in Supine Twist (Supta Matsyendrasana). Arms can be by your sides or extended out; gaze can be to the left, toward the sky, or to the right for a greater twist. Settle in and breathe naturally for 30 to 60 seconds, knowing that even the solid trees have twists and turns in their branches. Inhale, guiding the knees back to center, lift the hips just an inch, and exhale the hips back to center again. Uncross your legs and cross them with your left leg on top. Repeat Supine Twist on this side.

Staying on your back, step both feet on the sky in Legs Up the Wall Pose (Viparita Karani). Raise your arms toward your feet, take a gentle bend in your left leg as you draw your knee slightly toward your chest, and begin to practice gentle self-massage starting from the left foot, working down your left lower leg, making circles around your knee and along your thigh. After at least one minute, switch sides.

Return both feet to the sky, and begin to massage your arms, bringing the right hand to the back of the left hand and forearm, then to the palm side, and to the inner and outer wrists and forearms, gliding toward the armpit, shoulder, and chest. Take your time, and switch arms to repeat on the other side. Feel yourself melt into the mat. This inversion is safe for most people and can help release toxins and fluids from the lower limbs. Most of us don't receive a massage every day, and this is a beautiful way to give your*self* a massage. Chances are, you spend a great deal of time and energy caring for others. **You deserve to take at least a few moments each day to care for yourself.**

Lower both feet to the edges of the mat, allowing your knees to tilt inward and rest against each other, as your hands rest on your belly. Feel the natural rhythm of your breath: breathing in and expanding, breathing out and receding like waves in the ocean. Continue to breathe as you slide your hands up to your ribs, wrapping your thumbs toward your back ribs and your fingers around your front ribs. Inhale and feel not just your front ribs rise, but also your side ribs expand and your back press against the ground. Slide your hands up to the top of your chest/collarbone. Inhale and feel the top lobes of the lungs inflating, perhaps even the back of the heart melding into the mat. Breathe out, contracting.

Take several slow, mindful breaths. Keep one hand on your chest and bring the other hand to your belly. Go ahead and connect all three breaths, as if inflating one continuous balloon in the Three-Part/Complete Yogic Breath (Dirgha). Breathing in expands your belly, ribs, and chest;

breathing out, your chest recedes, your ribs contract, and your belly squeezes toward your spine. Continue breathing this way for 3-10 breath cycles.

Your body breathes automatically without you ever having to think about it, and yet you can also harness the power of your breath with mindful breathing, controlling your breath to regulate your own velocity, vol-

ume, and well-being. Returning to your natural breath, recall that *following the flow of your breath, the mind finds a natural place of rest.* Stay here, or straighten your legs for Deep Relaxation (Savasana) for a few more minutes, knowing that you charge most of your electronic devices daily. Why not take some time to recharge yourself?

As you're ready, begin to invite movement into your body by deepening your breath and wiggling your fingers/toes. Draw your knees toward your chest/ belly and rock side to side. Roll onto your left side and pause.

Press your right hand into the mat as you come up to sit. Thank you for taking time to slow down and to care for yourself.

Remember,

The peace of yoga,
Grounding and energizing,
Is with you always.

Namaste

9

"F" IS FOR FUN FAVORITES

(Meditation, Mindfulness, AWE, Yamas/Niyamas)

Meditation

What exactly is meditation and how do I know if I'm doing it right?

When I was in my late twenties, I dipped my toes into meditation by setting my alarm to wake myself before sunrise, sitting in a cross-legged position on the floor of my bedroom with my eyes closed, and focusing on my breath. Sometimes I would count the number of seconds for the inbreath and then count backwards for the outbreath. Other times I would focus on making the exhalation longer than the inhalation. I found that counting the breaths gave me something to occupy my busy mind during these early morning sessions. Invariably, my mind would wander, and I'd simply return to the breath. Eventually I worked up from just a few minutes of meditation to 20 or more minutes at a time, and the practice helped me to start the day with a calm and clear mind.

I couldn't tell you why or when I got away from my morning meditation practice—it just kind of slipped away. I guess that can happen with anything that's good for us if we're not intentional and disciplined about it—diet, exercise, learning something new . . . and yet, more than 20 years later, my studies led me to enroll in an advanced course on teaching meditation. Our instructor, Yoganand Michael Carroll, led the class on a wonderful exploration. Sitting in a circle, he asked the group, "What is meditation? If I sit on a cushion with my legs crossed and my eyes closed and chant the sound 'om', is that meditation?" Without any debate, we unanimously agreed that yes, that was meditation. "Now, if I stopped on my drive home from work to go for a peaceful walk in the woods, could that be meditation?" Again, without any real discussion, pretty much everyone nodded their head in agreement that, yes, a walk in the woods could be meditative.

"Okay," he continued, "If I fill the bath with warm water and add essential oils, and I slip into the water up to my neck and close my eyes, is that meditation?" There were some thoughtful expressions around the circle, but for the most part everyone agreed that this could be meditation. "And while I was in the tub, if I lit a candle to gaze upon and played some soft music, would this still be meditation?" Yes, we agreed, it surely would be. Stretching the envelope just a bit more, he asked, "What if I was enjoying my warm bath with essential oils, a candle and soft music, and I sipped a glass of wine at the same time?" This time there was a bit more rumbling among the group. After consideration, most of us agreed that it could still be meditative. Not satisfied, he pushed us further, "And what if I lit up a joint? Or listened to music by Pink Floyd or Kendrick Lamar? Would that still be meditation?" At this point, there was more heated debate amongst the group.

> Meditation is essentially focusing your attention mindfully.

Just what defines the boundaries of meditation anyway?

Spoiler alert: there were no exactly correct answers to our teacher's inquiries. It was becoming clearer that, just as "beauty is in the eye of the beholder," meditation can look, sound, smell, and feel different for different people under different circumstances. So how do you even know whether you're "doing it right"? At the end of the day, we all realized that meditation is essentially focusing your attention mindfully. This can include gazing at a candle, a piece of art, a sleeping child, or a drop of dew on a blade of grass. It can include awareness of scents like incense, essential oils, or just noticing the smell of your own skin. Meditation can happen in silence, or while listening to music, your heartbeat, or the sound of waves rolling in. It can happen in a place of worship, in nature, or in a busy airport. Meditation can be practiced while sitting, standing, lying down, walking, or moving mindfully in any way. It reminds me a bit of something Dr. Seuss might have written: "You can meditate in the rain, you can meditate on a plane, you can meditate here or there, you can meditate anywhere!"

Points to Ponder

- Considering your typical day, when might you incorporate a minute or more of meditation into your life? Think creatively here: Outside of setting your alarm to wake up earlier in the morning, could you take an extra minute in your daily shower to experience the sensation of the water? Could you pause when you pull your car into the garage and just breathe for a minute or so before entering your home? Can you take a break during your workday, even if it's on your way to the restroom, to listen to the sounds that surround you—the hum of a fan or the clicking of a keyboard? Write down at least two or more meditative possibilities that you can begin within the next 24 hours!

Mindfulness

The word "mindfulness" is becoming more common in everyday conversations. So what does it actually mean and what might that look like? The *New Oxford American Dictionary* gives two definitions of mindfulness:

1. The quality or state of being conscious or aware of something
2. A mental state achieved by focusing one's awareness on the present moment, while calmly acknowledging and accepting one's feelings, thoughts, and bodily sensations, used as a therapeutic technique

In a nutshell, *mindfulness is being aware in the present moment.* And yes, it can be very therapeutic! One of my favorite activities is what I call "Mindfulness in Motion," and there are endless ways to practice. A simple way to get started is the "Rainbow"—notice the colors of the rainbow in your natural environment. If you live in a crowded city or don't have ready access to nature, you can bring snippets of nature and color into your home with flowering plants (succulents don't require a great deal of space), or sharing your space with colorful fish or birds.

While walking outdoors, you can begin by looking for something red. Depending on where you're walking or what season it is, this can be a quick and easy exercise or a bit more challenging. Perhaps there are red berries or leaves, or even a red scab or bruise or bloodshot eye can count! Next you'll look for orange—again, this might look like flowers or leaves. For me, late in New England autumn, sometimes the only orange I can find is in the worn roots of trees, or even a streak of orangey-gold within a rock.

Move on to yellow—do you spy a bird with a yellow beak, or some green vegetation that went slightly yellow? Green can be just about anything growing outside, but can be trickier to find if you're living in a dry or desert region. Blue is many places, and often I lift my gaze to the sky. Someone once reminded me that even on a cloudy day, we know that there are blue skies up above the clouds.

Finally, we arrive at indigo and violet. If you wake up before sunrise and there isn't too much light pollution, the sky can be a deep and peaceful indigo glittering with the moon and stars. During daylight hours, you may spy an indigo berry or a purple hue in the vein of a leaf—be creative! This is a wonderful game to play with small children—basically a version of I Spy that encourages awareness and conversation, rather than handing them an electronic "babysitting" device. I guarantee that by practicing Mindfulness in Motion you will notice things you would have missed otherwise.

Mindfulness is being aware in the present moment.

Another fun favorite is scanning your surroundings as well as yourself for the Five Great Elements. Since āyurveda considers everything to be made up of the Five Elements, this can be practiced outside in nature or indoors. If you're trying to energize yourself, you may want to start from the ground up—moving from the solid, heavy Earth through Water, Fire, and Air, all the way up to light and subtle Space.

As an example in nature, Earth can be found in obvious places, like the ground you're walking on! Call to mind the qualities of Earth where you see them: rocks are dense, solid, stable, and heavy; dirt can be smooth, soft, dull, and cool.

Water can be obvious if you're near an ocean, lake, or stream, but where else might you find Water? Dew drops, ice and snow, fog and rain, and any other kind of moisture.

Fire is a radiant sun or glowing stars; it is piercing thorns and pine needles. Fire includes anything that is hot, sharp, penetrating, spreading, or smelly—that could even be found while cleaning up after your dog's "business"!

Air/Wind is certainly found in the breeze on your skin, and it is also found anywhere that you see movement: the current in a river, leaves fluttering in the wind, the movement of your body as your legs carry you step by step. While Air and Wind are subtle—they can't be seen—you can be mindful of the cooling effects of the wind, and how a stronger air flow can feel hard and rough against your face. Animals are in constant motion around you, whether they are mammals, birds, or insects.

Finally, you arrive at the element of Space. You might notice space between tree branches or above yourself/overhead. You can acknowledge the impact of your body moving through space, displacing the earth just a bit with each step, leaving subtle, clear, open space behind you. Inhale deeply and observe anything that arises for you.

Mindfulness is being aware in the present moment.

A variation of Five Great Elements practice that can be experienced outdoors or indoors is heightening your awareness of the elements within yourself. Again, you can start from the Earth and move your way up to Space if you'd like to lighten or uplift yourself, or you can practice top-down if you're wanting to wind down, calm, or ground yourself.

Starting with Space, become mindful of the spaces within your physical body: your eye sockets, sinuses, ear canals, mouth, lungs, digestive tract, and the lumens of your blood vessels that carry oxygen and nutrients to every cell in your body. Acknowledge that there are spaces between your cells and spaces within cells. Space allows potential.

Next you can consider Air/Wind in your body: each inhalation and every exhalation are an experience of air entering and exiting your body. Notice how the simple act of breathing moves your body, massaging your vital organs of digestion, elimination, and detoxification. Air/Wind are responsible for *all* movement: the flow of blood, the movement of food throughout the digestive system, and the conduction of all thoughts and nerve impulses in every cell.

Fire is evident anywhere that you feel heat: mouth, armpits, groin, and any areas of sharp pain or pulsating inflammation. Fire is responsible for digesting not only the foods you eat, but also processing sensory stimulation: making sense of the sounds, touches, sights, tastes, and smells that you experience. Fire includes your red blood cells that carry oxygen to each cell of your body.

Water includes your bodily fluids: tears that cleanse your eyes, saliva that moistens your mouth, synovial fluid that lubricates your joints, and cerebrospinal fluid that protects and nourishes your nervous system. Lymph and plasma escort toxins so they can be eliminated.

Earth is all that is heavy and stable: your bones are hard, steady, and solid (except the marrow and trabeculae contain space); your muscles are soft, dense, and smooth.

Inhale deeply and exhale slowly, noticing any thoughts or sensations that have shifted.

At the risk of repeating myself: *Mindfulness is being aware in the present moment.*

Cultivating mindfulness, especially through the elements, is a wonderful tool to increase self-awareness. Self-awareness leads to self-care, and self-care leads to self-compassion. By taking care of yourself, you become not only healthier yourself, but also more available to be present and caring for those around you, whether at work, at home, or in the community.

Points to Ponder

- When might you use mindfulness to better care for yourself? Could you do a morning element body scan to notice what you need in order to take care of yourself throughout the day? Could you practice the Rainbow technique as you walk around the block on your lunch break? Commit to at least one mindfulness practice this week by setting it on your calendar or as a reminder on your smartphone.

"AWE"

Positive psychology tells us that seeking awe-inspiring amazement, especially in the "small" experiences in life, can reap physical, psychological, and emotional benefits at any age. As a health care provider, you may have witnessed life at its bookends: birth and death. If you've ever parented or cared for young children, you may have witnessed the pure wonder and rapture that children have with their "firsts": first solid foods, first time feeling sand/grass/leaves/snow, and the grandeur, surprise, and excitement of taking their first steps! Animals can be excellent examples of practicing present-moment awareness and Awe, even as a puppy sniffs an interesting scent or a kitten bats around a piece of plastic or yarn.

"Awe is calming, settling, and grounding, but it also awakens and activates us. It makes us more open, curious, playful, and humorous."

Dacher Keltner, PhD, professor of psychology at the University of California, Berkeley, and social psychologist Jonathan Haidt, PhD, identified Awe's two key components: vastness and mystery. Being swept up in the beauty of music or visual art, being mesmerized by a sunrise or sunset, feeling sublime after a spiritual or meditative practice, and being open to receiving insight are all examples of feeling Awe.

In their book "The Power of Awe," Michael Amster, MD, and Jake Eagle, LPC, state that "Awe is calming, settling, and grounding, but it also awakens and activates us. It makes us more open, curious, playful, and humorous." To practice this method, they developed the easy-to-remember acronym, **AWE**:

- Pay **Attention**. Focus on something that catches your interest or inspires you—a drop of dew on a blade of grass, the sound of chimes in the wind, or the aroma of freshly brewed coffee.
- **Wait.** Pause to inhale deeply while staying present.
- **Exhale/Expand**. Concentrate on whatever feelings/sensations come up.

In the early stages of the pandemic, Amster and Eagle asked health care providers and members of the general community to practice AWE three times per day for as little as 15 seconds at a time—that's a whopping total of just under *one minute per day!* What they found was that both groups reduced symptoms of depression by 35 percent and anxiety by more than 20 percent. The beautiful thing is that it is absolutely free and has no negative side effects! And practicing this method of AWE is dose-dependent—the more you experience vastness and mystery, the greater the rewards in terms of overall well-being.

Points to Ponder

- What everyday experiences do you find to be inspirational or mesmerizing? Where might you experience even more AWE in life?

Yamas and Niyamas

In yogic tradition, there are five Yamas (Restraints) and five Niyamas (Observances). Here's where some people can start to feel a bit uncomfortable about yoga. Is it a religion? A cult? Some kind of crazy hippie shit? Elemental-Wellness blurs the lines between Western and traditional wisdom, *merging* them into a new wisdom. The word "merge" is defined by Wikipedia as the verb meaning "to blend or combine into a whole" and the noun meaning "the joining together of multiple sources." In this way, a new understanding *e-merges*. The word "emerge" derives from the Latin ēmergere, meaning "to rise out or up," which is a perfect description of what happens when two or more traditions coalesce.

Full disclosure, I was raised as a Roman Catholic, and for various reasons I don't go to church very often anymore. That being said, during my first year of undergraduate college at Fairfield University, a Jesuit Catholic institution, it was mandatory that we take Introduction to Religion. I'll never forget my professor, Reverend Simon Harak, a Jesuit priest. Not only did he teach us how to study, but he also introduced us to every major world religion. During the first class lecture, he asked us to privately identify one area of challenge or difficulty in our lives. Then he introduced us to a particular religious tradition, and our weekly assignment was to write a paper addressing our challenge from the point of view of a leader (priest, pastor, rabbi, etc.) from the religion of the week.

What I learned was that once you distill religions or belief systems down to their core tenets, pretty much all major religions have more in common than I'd realized. Most belief systems promote being a good and respectful person to yourself, your loved ones, and your neighbors or community, however you choose to define them. Don't steal, don't hurt others—these are fairly universal social norms.

Now I'm not out to anger anyone nor am I trying to change your religious beliefs or nonbeliefs. On the contrary, I'm introducing the Yamas and Niyamas here because I find they are a lovely complement to any belief system and they are useful in my daily life. As with everything that I offer, you are most welcome to take them or leave them. If you aren't familiar with Yamas and Niyamas, get curious and open your mind to new understanding. I'll explain what each word means, and then at the end, I'll share how I use the Yamas and Niyamas in my everyday life, and I'll offer suggestions as to how you might incorporate them, too. These are Sanskrit words that were originally passed down orally as opposed to written form, so the first is the most important and the other Restraints and Observances follow.

Yamas: Ahimsa, Satya, Asteya, Brahmacarya, and Aparigraha

Let's explore . . . **Ahimsa** means **non-harm, non-injury, nonjudgment** This would seem pretty straightforward, right? As health care providers, many of us took the Hippocratic Oath, which was derived from Greek medical texts, and requires a new physician/dentist/etc. to swear *by a number of healing gods (Oops! Did they tell you that in medical school?),* to uphold high standards and ethics. Much of what we practice today derives from ancient religious beliefs. I don't remember a single person in my combined University of Connecticut Medical and Dental School graduating class who ever questioned or objected to taking this oath in the name of a religious or philosophical conflict. Hopefully I can dispel the myth that we can't espouse values from another belief system, or that "cultural appropriation" is necessarily a negative thing. On the contrary, opening your mind to other traditions and incorporating positive and useful aspects leads to increased diversity, understanding, awareness, and acceptance. Perhaps a topic for another day, lest I digress!

As you know, the most important and basic message of the modern version of the Hippocratic Oath boils down to *Do no harm. "I will avoid twin traps of overtreatment and therapeutic nihilism."* Again, no problem. I think we can all get behind the concept of non-harm and non-injury—we all signed up to help people to be healthier and get better. But what about chemotherapy? That can be a fine line between benefitting your patients and harming them. And what about side effects to drugs and surgical complications? Yes, the medication may lower your blood pressure, and it may also contribute to gingival hyperplasia and systemic inflammation, which contribute to hypertension and cardiovascular disease.

Hmmm . . . okay, perhaps you can see that this becomes a bit trickier than it looked at first glance, since these are definitely ethical considerations. And what about that *nonjudgment* piece? That can be a bit stickier. Do you judge patients who are noncompliant with your recommendations? Do you judge your coworkers for their efforts, abilities, or lack thereof? Do you judge yourself harshly or unfairly in ways that you wouldn't judge your colleagues? Do you judge family members for leaving their socks on the floor or not taking out the trash? What about your friends? Community? There's so much to think about here that Ahimsa could make up an entire chapter of this book.

Moving on to the second Yama, **Satya**, which means **truth**. Again, veracity is part of our oath. We agree to tell the truth to our patients, and hopefully you are also truthful in your personal life. Informed consent requires that you educate patients regarding treatment options, risks, and benefits so that they may make informed choices. Even if you don't personally offer a particular procedure and might need to refer the patient to another provider, you still inform the patient of what is possible in order to relay the truth.

Overtreatment is another ethical dilemma. For example, what happens when a young, healthy patient with no history of dental decay presents to my office with minor spaces or tooth size discrepancies in her front teeth, and she requests that I fabricate 10 veneers so that she has a beautiful, straight, white smile? With my knowledge, skills and talents, I can easily provide this service and generate a significant profit. However, I am *truth*ful when I explain that another option might include some minor bonding procedures or limited orthodontics with whitening at a fraction of the cost to the patient. This is a much more conservative approach and I would argue a more appropriate, less costly, and less invasive option, even though I could benefit more financially if I simply honored her initial request without educating her regarding the risks and benefits of all options.

And what about a minor medical error? If there was a complication during a procedure and you were able to "fix" the problem without the patient's knowledge, it's still necessary to inform the patient about what happened, including any potential ramifications or future considerations.

Another example is a patient with an existing history of congestive heart failure, COPD, and stage four prostate cancer who contracts a respiratory virus. Due to respiratory complications, he is subsequently hospitalized and later succumbs. What is his cause of death? Is it solely the virus? Or would it be more *truth*ful to include his other pre-existing conditions as contributors to his death?

And what about your communication with others in your personal and professional life? Do you speak clearly and directly, or do you "triangulate"—gossip or talk to someone else about a conflict rather than speaking directly to the person with whom you have an issue? Are you honest about your feelings and your physical and mental wellness?

After severely injuring my dominant shoulder and recovering from the necessary surgical reconstruction, I had to be honest with myself, my coworkers, and my patients. I wasn't strong enough and didn't have the physical/neurological coordination or mental stamina to perform all procedures or even work a full day at first. I needed to ask for help. I had to hire an associate dentist to restore lower molars because it wasn't safe yet for me to do so, which brings us back to number one: *Ahimsa—do no harm*. Besides being truthful in your work and in your personal relationships (saying you'll do something but not following through versus being a person of integrity who is true to your word), Satya also means being honest with yourself. Are you keeping up with continuing education in order to provide the best care to your patients? Are you taking care of yourself to the best of your ability? Getting restful sleep? Eating nutritiously? Practicing self-care? As you can see, being *truth*ful impacts every aspect of your life.

Next comes **Asteya, or nonstealing**. I'm assuming here that you are not in the habit of shoplifting or breaking and entering into your neighbor's home. As you may be starting to realize, these values run deeper than that. At work, do you sit around and have personal conversations while you're "clocked in," rather than saving longer conversations for your break time? This is stealing time and wages from your employer. If you're working as a dental hygienist, do you sometimes take extra samples home for your personal use? All of this is worth thinking about because, as the saying goes, "How you do anything is how you do everything." Here, integrity and mindfulness go hand in hand. Any time that you take more than your fair share (from a buffet line or from a vendor at a convention hall or from a Halloween goody bag!), you are violating the principle of Asteya.

One of the most precious resources is time, and it's not renewable. When you're having any conversation, what percent of the time are you speaking or thinking about your response to what the other person is saying, versus being present and listening to what they're truly expressing? In my daily practice, I often think of Asteya in terms of *presence*. Whether they're my family, my pets, my patients, my employees, or the cashier at the grocery store register, am I truly present with the person in front of me? With the busy-ness of life—running from one activity or patient to another—practicing *presence* can be one of the biggest challenges of the day. In the midst of caring for a patient, do you ever find yourself daydreaming about what you're going to eat for dinner or thinking about your weekend plans? If and when this happens, you can exhale your distraction, and with the next inhalation you can reorient your attention and awareness back to the present person, place, and time. Personally, I struggle with being present with myself and honoring time that I've set aside as downtime or self-care. It's so easy to just work a little harder or do one more thing, rather than honor the time that I had planned to enjoy a jigsaw puzzle or snuggle up with the dogs and a good book. Asteya is a daily work in progress!

Brahmacarya refers to **energy management.** Thousands of years ago, this referred to observing the life of an ascetic monk, with the routine of meditating for hours on end, bringing you closer to enlightenment (or escapism—life was pretty harsh back then!). As "householders" in the 21st century, energy management corresponds to living a good life, with habits that make you a good person and a contribution to society.

For me, I'm most mindful of energy management on the days that I wake up feeling stressed or scattered even before I leave the house in the morning. With the awareness that my energy is a bit frenetic, I remind myself to manage my energy by becoming more grounded (for example, by practicing meditation or calming breathing techniques, by practicing yoga and journaling, and by setting my intentions or positive affirmation for the day). When snafus invariably arise, I remind myself that the problem is not personal. The issue is just "a thing" and I can manage myself by breathing slowly down toward my belly. Energy management can be as simple as not flying off the handle when you're stuck in traffic or something irritates you.

The fifth Yama is **Aparigraha**, the Restraint of **detachment,** or **being unattached to people, places, and outcomes.** As health care providers, there are situations when the patient's health outcome isn't what we'd hoped for—they didn't respond to treatment as expected and their health has continued to deteriorate, or they fell out of the loop and discontinued their care with you, either transferring to another provider or abandoning their treatment plan. At these moments, you realize that there are many factors that are beyond your control. While you can educate and influence your patient toward what you consider to be the ideal treatment path, the Principle of Autonomy dictates that the choice is ultimately up to the patient. You can't enforce their compliance with diet and exercise recommendations or even taking medication as prescribed, unless they are in a controlled environment. Even in a controlled situation, you can't force someone to comply with physical therapy; they've got to want to do the work.

After my mother-in-law suffered a fall that resulted in a hip fracture and surgical joint replacement, she was prescribed the necessary physical therapy. Despite the fact that just a few years prior she had been an avid walker and enjoyed riding a bicycle, her pre-existing dementia made it difficult for her to understand the necessity of rehab, and she lacked the physical strength and mental capacity to ever walk again. For the family who loved her and wanted the best for her, this was difficult to accept, and yet it was necessary to let go of attachment to the outcome. Mental health, addiction rehabilitation, and cancer treatments are areas where we see relapse more often than we'd like to, and yet health care providers can only do the best that we can do.

At both ends of the spectrum, in pediatrics and geriatrics, it's common to see *overattachment* in terms of "helicopter parenting" (overcontrolling parents who speak for the child when the child is capable of answering for themself) and "hovering adult children" (adult children who may or may not have power of attorney over their parents and attempt to control their parents' lives—where they live, what they eat, what medical treatment plan they pursue). For example, this can be an ethical conflict when adult children call and ask to discuss their parent's treatment plan without having written consent from the patient. In my practice, well-meaning adult children (who did not accompany their fully independent and cognizant parent to their appointment) have called with questions about the difference between oral appliance therapy/mandibular advancement splints versus continuous positive air pressure (CPAP) to treat obstructive sleep apnea. Without having permission to speak about their parent's medical history, I can only answer general questions and educate them on the risks and benefits of both options (knowing that their mother does not tolerate and will not use CPAP).

Overattachment can happen in other relationships. Have you ever witnessed a friend (of course, it's never yourself) who stayed in a personal relationship for far too long? Abusive and toxic relationships are the most obvious examples of being stuck in an unhealthy relationship, but what about the relationships that are one-sided? You know, the "friend" who only calls when she needs something from you, or the "friend" who is great at dumping all their troubles on you but not so good at reciprocating when you need a helping hand or compassionate ear.

At work, there can be mismatches in philosophy between employer/institution and employee. Are you employed with someone who is unethical? It can be as simple as an office that isn't observing sterilization or privacy protocols. As a dental hygienist, are you working in an office that hasn't kept up to date with periodontal protocols, or working for a dentist who "watches" conditions that you identify as active dental disease or suspicious lesions that warrant biopsy? If you're experiencing a significant conflict in *values*, whether in your personal or professional relationships, that may be a reason to reconsider your level of attachment and commitment.

And what about places and situations? You may have known friends or family members (again, it's never yourself) who have complained for years about how miserable they are in their place of work, but they stay because the pain of change (searching for and obtaining more suitable work) feels greater than the discomfort of staying. Finding a new job requires going outside their comfort zone, potentially learning new skills, and feeling vulnerable. But the rewards of health, growth, and happiness may be well worth the effort!

I discussed attachment to places and things in the section on the doshas as a *kapha imbalance*. While hoarding is an obvious example of overattachment, so is holding onto things that no longer bring you joy or—even worse!—energetically drain you. Keeping a gift that adds to your sense of weight and clutter rather than passing it along or donating it to someone who might use or enjoy it more; holding onto clothing that is many times too small for you or way outdated because you think you'll lose weight and get back into it again; hanging onto that bread machine/air fryer/crockpot/blender/fill-in-the-blank that you haven't used in years because it could come in handy one day—are all examples of overattachments to things. As you can see, Aparigraha encompasses many aspects of life!

Niyamas: Saucha, Santosha, Tapas, Svadhya-ya, and Isvara Pranidhana

The first Niyama, or Observance, is **Saucha,** which means **cleanliness**. What comes to mind here—keeping a clean home, workspace, and personal hygiene? Beyond basic cleanliness, clearing clutter, having a semblance of organization, and managing your schedule and your calendar responsibly are all examples of cleanliness. When was the last time you cleared your desk or cleaned out your closets? You might find that removing clutter helps you to feel lighter and opens space for creativity.

What about the foods you eat? Circling back to the doshas, are you **FLOSS**ing? Eating a diet that is primarily *fresh, local, organic, seasonal, and sustainable* is considered to be "eating clean." Or are you eating fast foods on the run, grabbing whatever you can find in the vending machine or convenience market? Do you enjoy caffeine and alcohol in moderation (or not at all)? Consider small ways that you can enhance your life right now. When might you be able to prepare food so that you know you'll have some healthy options for the week? If getting to the grocery store on your day off just doesn't happen, can you swing by on a lunch break or visit a farmer's market on your way home from work? How could you cut back your sugar/refined carbohydrate consumption even 5 to 10 percent? Could you try substituting a "nightcap" with a cup of herbal tea instead? The options are limitless, and the rewards can be amazing!

Moving onto the second Niyama, **Santosha** means **contentment** While I'm a big fan of the Japanese concept of *kaizen,* or *continuous improvement,* Santosha refers to *contentment with what is,* even while striving to grow and improve. Far from promoting complacency, Santosha commands radical acceptance, happiness with what is, and loving yourself just the way you are in the present moment. Santosha is like a parent's unconditional love: yes, they want to see their child grow and develop and not throw tantrums like a toddler at the age of 21, and unconditional love implies that they accept exactly who and how their child is in this very moment.

Santosha sounds like, "I'm trying to learn this new skill/language/recipe/procedure and I'm not very good at it yet, but I acknowledge the effort I've made and I love who I am." This one can be a nice reminder for the overachievers—you know, those of us who are prone to pitta imbalances and hypercriticism of self and others. Ask yourself, "Can I be okay with my life, my situation, myself exactly the way things are in this moment?" Seriously, right now, soften your gaze or close your eyes and ask yourself, *"Can I be okay with my life, my situation, myself exactly the way things are in this moment?"* Now stay with that thought for a few moments and feel what that feels like in your body. Is there any sense of softening around your eyes or jawline? Have your shoulders relaxed just a little bit? Maybe yes, maybe not. Whatever you experience is uniquely yours. And the more you practice Santosha, the greater your potential to experience *Bliss, Not Burnout.*

Next comes **Tapas, or Uplifting Discipline.** Since these principles were originally passed along orally (as opposed to being written down), as I already mentioned, the Restraints and Observances that come first are most important. It's interesting that Tapas follows Santosha In other words, you could say that it's considered more important to be content and love yourself first, just the way that you are, before you attempt to improve yourself. And then there is uplifting discipline!

Tapas is the Observance that reminds us to do the things that help us to grow, improve, and progress, even when we don't feel like it. Tapas was the discipline to attend class, to study in school, and to learn the necessary skills to become a health care provider. Tapas is going to bed at a reasonable hour and setting your alarm to get up and meditate, exercise, pray, journal, or otherwise prepare for your day. Uplifting discipline means that you're not a quitter—you pick yourself up after a setback and try again, acknowledging the experience as a learning process as opposed to a failure. Tapas is declining a third helping of mashed potatoes at the holiday meal in favor of taking a 10-minute walk to digest what you've already eaten.

The fourth Niyama is **Svadhya-ya,** or **Self-Awareness.** At the Kripalu center, where I studied yoga and āyurveda, it is said that *"Self-observation without judgment is the highest form of practice."* The fact that you are reading this section at this very moment in time is a testament to the fact that you are interested in at least some level of reflection and self-awareness. The whole purpose of recognizing your dosha, or constitutional makeup, is so that you have greater awareness and can make choices that support your well-being, as well as recognize your tendencies to fall off track and intervene on your own behalf (and the behalf of people around you!).

Self-awareness is necessary in order to navigate and be aware of others. Have you ever noticed that individual who just didn't seem to "read the room"? You know, that obnoxiously loud talker at a concert, movie theater, or fine dining restaurant? In these situations you can see that sometimes lack of self-awareness can appear to be self-absorption. Svadhya-ya circles back to Santosha: Can you be aware of yourself in the present moment and accept who you are with love? When self-reflection reveals an area of weakness or potential for improvement, you can draw upon Tapas or Uplifting Discipline to make the necessary changes or implement growth opportunities.

So how do you become more self-aware? Everything about this book is designed to offer strategies for increased awareness and well-being. Being aware of your makeup and tendencies, practicing some form of reflective mindfulness/meditation/prayer/journaling, using reflection and embodiment (through yoga, exercise, mindfulness, breathing techniques, etc.) to become present with yourself, living your life with intention and on purpose—these are all ways to be more present, embodied, and self-aware. What you do with the information of awareness is up to you! What I can tell you, though, is that practicing awareness and self-awareness gets you closer to *Bliss* and further from *Burnout*.

Last, but not exactly least, the final Niyama is **Îsvara Pranidhana,** or **Trust.** Trusting *tat and sat,* Sanskrit for that which is *real and true.* After admitting that you need help, the backbone of a 12-step recovery program is accepting and *trusting in something greater than yourself.* When you put in all the right ingredients, whether it's designing and delivering a patient's treatment plan or surgery, raising your children, or creating and serving a new holiday dish for the very first time, Îsvara Pranidhana means that you relinquish control of the outcome, and trust that you have done enough and that there truly are forces beyond your influence that are greater than yourself (again, the precise entity varies—some call it God or the equivalent in their belief system, Nature, the Universe, Community, Energy—whatever that force is and whatever it means to *you*).

Trust means that even when you prepare for the worst, you hope for and believe in a positive result. Trust mixes in a bit of Aparigraha, or detachment, and it allows life to unfold as it should. Regardless of what happens, practicing Îsvara Pranidhana is an exercise in knowing that, no matter what, you are already whole and complete and you will be okay. Living with trust relieves some of the stresses and burdens of life, because you can't carry them all yourself and you certainly can't control them. For all you overachieving perfectionists, here is your opportunity to exhale!

So how do you put this all together and how can the Yamas and Niyamas be used in everyday life? When I was first studying these concepts, I would focus on just one of the 10 Restraints/Observances for a period of five days or a week. For example, the first week I practiced Ahimsa, non-harm/non-injury/nonjudgment. I made a point to check in with myself throughout the day, and then again at the end of the day, to see where I had practiced the concept and also when I had found it challenging to do so. By staying with just one practice at a time, I was able to get well-acquainted with each one. These days, I choose at least one Yama and one Niyama each day and fold them into my daily intention or affirmation as I'm journaling. The possibilities are endless.

Points to Ponder

- Could you commit to practicing just one Yama or Niyama for a week at a time, just as a little experiment, and see how it goes? If you like the practice, you can incorporate the exercise into your daily routine. If you don't like it, well, you still tried something new, and for that you can be proud of yourself!

Discussion of Yamas and Niyamas is a lot, and you may need a mental stretch break before we dive into the final chapter. Go ahead, seriously. Get yourself a drink of water, go for a little walk, pet your cat, stretch your arms and yawn, or just put this book down and come back to it in a bit when you're refreshed and ready to carry on!

Alternatively, if you are primed and ready to go, let's hit it! Your choice, always . . .

10

"G, H, I, J" ARE FOR GRATITUDE AND GRACE, HARMONY, INTENTIONALITY, AND JOURNALING

Gratitude can be an antidote for so many "unpleasant" feelings: anxiety, depression, stress, etc. Considering constitutional (doshic) imbalances, we've already covered the negative health ramifications of allowing these feelings to run amuck: unhealthy weight loss or gain, arthritis, ulcers, rashes, digestive disorders, predisposition to cancers and heart disease—just to name a handful! So how can writing words on a piece of paper or just being thankful help?

"Where the mind goes, energy flows."

Journaling in general offers so many possibilities. It's not your thing, you say? You're so busy that you couldn't add a single extra task to your day? You've tried it and it doesn't "work" for you? I once had a woman share that when she was going through her divorce, her therapist recommended that she write in a journal, so she dutifully did. What she found was that it just reinforced her feelings of anger, frustration, and hurt, and it ended up compounding her pain. Understandably so! Instead of providing a release or catharsis of stress and pain, she was focusing on her feelings of pain, frustration, and anger.

There is a saying in yoga and mindfulness practice that "Where the mind goes, energy flows." In performance training, it's called "target focus," and it's why race car drivers never ever look at the wall, but instead keep their eyes on the road ahead. It stands to reason that if you continuously play and replay negative thoughts and imagery, you will continue to attract and experience precisely the things that you don't want in your life. The flip side of the coin is that when you focus on what is going well, what is good and "right," what you desire *as if you already have it,* you attract positivity and more of what you do want in your life.

How do you go from complaining about everything that's going wrong to proclaiming and claiming your best life? Simply by making the transition. In order to make any shift, first you must meet yourself precisely where you are. Acknowledging and accepting your current reality is imperative, and what you do with that reality is the crucial next step.

Once you've allowed the emotions to be expressed, it's time to breathe and take a healthy step back. What would it look like if you viewed your situation with a bit of distance? Sometimes it can be helpful to consider how you would speak to a beloved friend in a similar situation. More often than not, this takes some of the self-judgment away and broadens your view and perspective. Now take a further step back. With a little more space, how does the situation appear? Do more possibilities exist than you initially realized? Practicing being a witness or observer brings greater clarity and can help you to move from negativity to positivity.

Melody is a medical assistant who describes her ideal workday as "being fully staffed, unrushed, and feeling respected" by her boss. One day she found herself being the only person covering a four-person job. In the past, feeling depleted and overwhelmed at work would lead her to drink alcohol as a means to relieve stress. When she found that this wasn't working well for her, she stopped drinking and began exercising/working out and going to bed earlier to get more rest. By taking better care of herself inside and outside of her work environment, she was able to collect herself on a potentially stressful day and get "mentally prepared." She consciously became more focused on patient care and flow so that she and the doctor could stay on time for patients. She worked efficiently and directed some patients to a portal for their visit summary. At the end of the day, she felt calm and accomplished, having stayed present and on time for both doctor and patients.

How did Melody's strategies work for her? It would be understandable for anyone to feel frantic in the face of having to do the work of four people (of course, for the pay of one!). No one would have judged her harshly if she had become short-tempered, impatient, frustrated, and resentful. She could have thrown up her hands and gotten angry. She could have taken it out on the patients and vented about how there's never enough help and how she's overworked and underpaid. She could have told herself that the day was going to be a "nightmare," that she'd never be able to take care of all the patients or stay on time, and that the schedule would be a disaster. She could have spiraled down into a deep, dark hole of blame, negativity, and self-pity, none of which would have helped her situation.

Instead of ranting, complaining, and catastrophizing, she assessed the situation, exhaled, and grounded and centered herself. She shifted her mindstate to available solutions and possibilities. Fortunately, her self-care outside of work helped Melody to *pause* and consider the situation with a different *perspective*. At the end of the day, while she was tired, she didn't feel depleted and actually felt a sense of accomplishment for having done her best.

And *that* is what journaling offers—the ability to step back to view the bigger picture. Rather than wallowing in your mental and emotional filth, journaling provides one strategy to bathe your feelings and don a fresh mental attitude. Doing this regularly in writing trains you to be able to do so in any moment—in real time and space.

There are infinite ways to keep a journal. Some individuals opt to use an app that suggests some "thought starters." Others enjoy a paper journal with written reflections or writing prompts. And some people are writing-averse—they just think it's not their thing. And you know what? Lots of things that are good for you may not be your thing, like eating healthy, exercising, brushing, and flossing your teeth—honestly, who loves to do these things every single day, day after day? Even as a dentist myself, there are some nights I just don't feel like flossing, but I know I need to and it's good and healthy for me, so I do it.

The same can be said for journaling: if you don't currently have a habit of regular journaling, perhaps you could consider adding it in very small baby steps. Do you truly not have even *one* minute when you could reflect either at the beginning or end of your day? Get creative—could you do it on the toilet in the morning? While taking public transportation, walking, or waiting at a red light on your morning commute? There's really not one best way to journal. Yes, I prefer written journaling without other distractions, as I believe there is a kinesthetic advantage to physically writing out your thoughts and feelings with undivided attention. But that's not the only way and it's not for everyone. If you currently have no journaling habit, how would it be if you started your morning by making notes on your phone or in a small notebook—just becoming aware of how you're feeling in the moment and setting an intention for the coming day? How might your day unfold differently?

In Melody's scenario, she didn't have a specific journaling practice, but she clearly used exercise, sleep, and mindfulness to be *intentional* about her day. If she wants to strengthen her ability to be mindful and intentional, journaling is an inexpensive tool that can help. So how would you begin? Again, baby steps are the best way to set yourself up for success. At first, you might not journal every day. Perhaps there are days when you have more time (like a day off) than a busy work day.

And when is the best time to journal? The short answer (as with flossing your teeth!) is the time that you're most likely to do it. There are benefits to journaling at the end of your day: processing the day's events, recognizing what worked well and celebrating it, acknowledging what didn't go the way you'd hoped, and considering how you might approach the situation differently in the future. Evening is also a beautiful time to reflect on that for which you are grateful, and it's also the perfect time to prepare for the coming day.

On the other hand, beginning your day with reflection, mindfulness, and intentionality can be incredibly powerful to set yourself up for the day. Morning practice can begin with affirmations that you can utilize throughout the day as a beacon of light and an anchor to ground yourself if things begin to unravel.

For others, taking time over a lunch break to journal can be a wonderful way to clear the mind and reset for the remainder of their day. With regular practice, you just might find that journaling can be helpful in unexpected ways, and you may be drawn to journaling more often!

Let's get down to the "nitty gritty." Here I'll share with you the nuts and bolts of my personal journaling practice. The process has developed over years, and I take anywhere from 10 minutes or less on a busy morning to a glorious 40 minutes or more on a luxurious day off. My practice has evolved over time—at first, it was shorter and more simplistic. That's a great way to start. You may find that after a period of regular journaling, you might want to add extras to your practice to expand the "routine."

I personally prefer to journal in the morning. I get out of bed ideally before the sun rises, hydrate, stretch/yoga/breathe/meditate, and *then* sit down with my favorite warm beverage to journal. The hydrating and yoga prepare me mentally and physically to be in a more clear, alert, and reflective frame of mind. If you have an hour or more, fantastic! If you literally have 10 minutes, then do what you can for yourself in that amount of time. I actually begin with a salutation of "Good morning!" I'm still not sure to whom I'm speaking—perhaps the universe in my case. It could be to your higher power, a friend, a mentor, a family member, or even yourself. Something about that opener tells me that I've arrived at journal time, kind of like a centering practice before I begin yoga or meditation. From there, I just write how I'm feeling—mentally, physically, emotionally. Some days I feel energetic, other days I wish I was getting back in bed. There's no right or wrong here, there's just what is real and true for you. From there, I move on to three reflections on the previous day:

1. What did I learn? (Or where did I improve or progress?) This could be something you learned from a class, a book, a documentary, or any other source. It could be trying a new recipe, hobby, or walking path. Sometimes learning something new can be catching up with an old friend and listening to what's new/going on in their life. The goal is to learn, grow, or improve on a daily basis as a means to continual growth. If you can't think of anything, it's an opportunity to consider what growth opportunities might be available in the coming day.

2. How did I make a difference? This could be anything! Did you surgically remove someone's cancer? Did you hold someone's hand? Did you look into your patient's eyes (or your partner's, child's, parent's, or a complete stranger's eyes) and give them the gift of being seen and heard—humanized? Did you smile at someone who was having a rough day? Did you hold the door for someone or let someone into the flow of traffic?

    Whether literally lifesaving or seemingly small, every kind act has the potential to have the ripple effect. You tipped the barista at the coffee shop? Perhaps that acknowledgement encouraged them to continue to serve with joy and enthusiasm. Did you recognize a coworker's need for help and step in without them even asking you to pitch in? They will appreciate your support, and possibly be more present and compassionate toward your mutual patients, as well as more likely to help you in the future. Did you call or send a thoughtful text to a friend or loved one, just to say that you're thinking of them and that you care? If you're even thinking about it, they need to hear from you! Your message may arrive at precisely the moment they are in need of support. Again, making a difference doesn't have to seem earth-shattering—even the smallest acts of kindness count!

3. What insights came up? This one can be a bit trickier at first, so let's look at some examples. For starters, I've actually started writing this book three times (and stopped twice!) over the course of the last several years. Each time, I'd get going, and then something would get in the way. I'd have creative writer's block ("I just don't know what to write next.") or imposter syndrome ("I'm not a writer or an author. Who am I to think I can write this book? I'm not good enough. Who will want to read this anyway? It's just a waste of time."). Or life would get in the way. (My mother was hospitalized and needed help, so I paused writing. I had injuries/surgical procedures that would interfere. Or some other excuse.)

I've had the mindset that writing a book is a daunting task, that it is difficult and arduous and I don't know when I'll ever complete the project. But this third time's the charm! I was simultaneously reading multiple books while I was writing. Brené Brown inspired me to be conversational. Tricia Brouk and Dr. Alexandra Stockwell coauthored *The Invitation*, a book about menopause, by recording their intentional conversation over the course of a weekend and then having someone else transcribe their conversation into a book. What a creative and ingenious idea! Reading *Sleep Interrupted* by Steven Park, MD, provided a model of medical writing that is accessible to people of different backgrounds.

Suddenly my insight was that my mindset was getting in my own way. Once I realized that and shifted my mindstate, I had a whole new approach! Deciding that the process could be fun and flow naturally helped me to gather momentum, and I began to look forward to writing more regularly. I found joy, versus anxiety, in the process.

You could also choose to implement *some* of the exercises offered in the previous pages. Let's say that you tried getting up 20 minutes earlier so you could stretch for 10 minutes and journal as well. After trying this for a few weeks, your insight may be that taking time for yourself first thing in the morning helps you to have a better day. Or your insight may be that you're completely *not* a morning vāta person and that you'd benefit more from enjoying those last 20 minutes of sleep. If that sounds like you, I encourage you to give it an honest try! Any change may not reap immediate results. Going on a calorie-restricted diet and exercise regimen isn't going to cause you to drop a ton of weight in a day—some things take time and consistent practice to appreciate the benefits, so try to stick with any positive change for three weeks before assessing your results.

A shorter version combining the first three reflection points could simply be *What was good and positive about my day? With hindsight, what might I have done differently?* These two questions are great if you have less time for journaling. **Always** start with the positives! The things that you might do differently are your potential growth points. It's not about critiquing yourself. If, at the end of the day (or first thing in the morning, if you choose to journal then), you realize that you've been running around in a million directions and you're completely exhausted and cranky, you can consider how you might approach things differently in order to support your well-being.

This might mean saying no to someone's requests. Perhaps you realize that you didn't really need to do all the errands or work projects in one day. You might need to ask for help, like creating a carpool so you're not driving all over in addition to doing your work responsibilities. Hiring help with chores at home (house cleaner, landscaper, meal delivery, etc.) may free up some time and relieve stress if it's an option financially. Or you might find that slowing down just a little and taking time for yourself reaps more benefits than you ever imagined!

4. *What made me laugh?* The National Institutes of Health states that children laugh about *400* times per day, whereas the average adult laughs only about *15* times. Personally, I want to live a life full of joy and wellness! Not every second of every day is going to be a party, of course. I focus on the things that make me happy—perhaps where I bring out someone's smile or brighten their day—in order to have more of these experiences.

    Where the mind goes, energy flows. The more you reinforce the positives, the more positivity will come your way. You can connect with people by making eye contact and acknowledging them. When you're interacting with a waiter or customer service representative or maintenance worker, call them by name and engage them personally. This could look like asking them how their day is going, thanking them for taking time and being patient in answering your questions, and appreciating them for keeping the restroom clean. In my daily work as a dentist, I often share a corny dentist joke or funny story with a patient to get them to relax a little. Personally, texting a pun or play on words about the daily Wordle puzzle to my son makes us both smile. The smallest gestures can have a huge impact when it comes to humanizing another person and uplifting them.

5. *For what am I grateful?* This one is nonnegotiable! As trite as the phrase "an attitude of gratitude" may seem, practicing **gratitude** regularly is an absolute must! If you can't think of *at least* three things for which you are grateful,

that's cause for even greater reflection. Whether it's a roof over your head, a warm beverage in the morning, clean water to drink, or simply waking up alive one more day, there are infinite reasons to give thanks.

Giving thanks doesn't need to be relegated to one day a year at the Thanksgiving dinner table. When our children were barely verbal, we would each take turns at the dinner table sharing three things that were good about our day and for which we were grateful. Speaking your appreciation solidifies the experience. You also give the other person something to consider that they might not have thought of on their own, and their thanks may inspire you to recognize additional blessings.

Some people keep a separate gratitude journal. You can certainly reflect on things for which you are grateful as you lay your head to rest on your pillow at night. And yet there is something very powerful about physically writing out these gifts. It makes them real and tangible, they can be referenced and repeated. *Mindfulness manifests.*

6. *I'm looking forward to . . .* Bringing to mind that which will bring you joy later in the day lifts you up just by imagining it! Some days you may be looking forward to helping a particular patient or accomplishing a challenging procedure. Other days you may joyfully anticipate catching up with a friend on your commute to work, walking your dog, playing with your children to wind down after a long day, or spending time with your favorite person, hobby, or book before bed. On the most difficult days, I still look forward to enjoying a shower and some herbal tea, as well as being back home in my own bed at night. When the day gets tough, you can always recall that which you were looking forward to.

7. *A potential challenge or snafu could be . . .* This I credit to motivational and personal development trainer Brendon Burchard. Why in the world would you want to think about what could go wrong? Flight crews prepare for crash landings. Surgical teams prepare for potential complications. First responders learn how to handle any obstacle that presents itself in any given moment.

By anticipating where things *could* go astray, you give yourself space to plan strategies for managing obstacles. For instance, if you know you might need to work late and may not make it to daycare before closing time, you might arrange for a family member, neighbor, or friend to pick up the kids for you. If you anticipate traffic due to forecasted heavy rain, you can plan to leave earlier or take a different route. If you know you have a challenging patient on the day's schedule, you can brainstorm ways to make the visit go better, or at least take care of yourself so you support yourself and bring your best to the situation.

8. *Who will I serve?* Obviously, as a health care provider you are in the health care *service* industry, which means that you get to serve every single patient with

whom you interact. Maybe when you realize that it's a patient's birthday, you can give them a card or some flowers, or a small token/gift card. You can plan to treat your coworker to their favorite coffee or lunch.

On the personal side, you can plan to surprise your partner with fresh flowers or some big or small gift. Every act of kindness counts! It could be as simple as doing a favor or taking out the trash without being asked, and this is your opportunity to get creative and have fun. You'll probably notice that just thinking about doing something nice for someone else brings a smile to your own face! Now you get to think about this throughout the day, feeling joyful yourself. That's a win-win: you feel good anticipating serving someone, and then you feel good when it actually happens. (And hopefully the recipient is appreciative. However, a true gift or act of kindness is done without attachment to the outcome or the receiver's reaction.)

9. *Set an **intention** and/or state an affirmation.* This is powerful. Stating "I am . . ." is a strong declaration. When you complete the statement with something positive, such as "I am loving and present," "I am clear and intentional," or "I am calm and centered," you are proclaiming to yourself and the universe exactly who you are in the world.

That's fine and dandy, you may say, but exactly how do you come up with your intention or affirmation? As always, I'm so glad you asked that! Most importantly, feel free to do whatever works best for you. Personally, I reflect on the yogic traditions of the Yamas and Niyamas, which translate into Restraints and Observances. I included these in the "Fun Favorites" in Chapter 9. When you are reflective at the beginning of your day, either with yoga/stretching, prayer, meditation, journaling, gazing at the sunrise, or engaging in any other reflective activity, you'll have a sense of what you need to remember most as you start a new day.

For instance, if I feel myself feeling sluggish and foggy brained but I know I need to be alert for a busy day at the office, I might choose the Yama Asteya for "nonstealing" (to me this is also about not stealing other people's time and attention, or simply being *present* with whomever needs my attention in each moment). I might choose the Niyama Tapas for uplifting discipline. Even when I don't feel like doing something that truly needs to be done, I can remind myself of why it's important and "just do it." Then these can all be combined into one intentional affirmation, like "I am uplifting, present, and clearly focused." Again, stating your intention as "**I am** . . ." is a powerful energetic statement.

Let's say you wake up feeling scattered and anxious about a big case or presentation, or something that's happening in your personal life outside of work. As discussed in the section on the doshas, anxiety is an example of a vāta overload imbalance—essentially too much Air (Wind) and Space. How could you use the Yamas, Niyamas, and elements to help set an intention that could best serve you for the day?

You'll recall that we balance imbalances by choosing the opposite qualities. You might choose the Yama Brahmacarya (energy management) to remind yourself not to spiral out of control; you could choose the Niyama Svadhya-ya (self-awareness) to remind yourself to be mindful of your energy throughout the day. You can scan the elements for balance: stability of Earth > Mobility of Wind, and the gross, concrete qualities of Earth > Subtlety of Wind. Combining these, you can intentionally affirm "I am grounded and embodied." The possibilities are limitless! And there is no right or wrong way to set an intention/affirmation. The goal is to choose what supports you the most.

So where does *"Harmony"* fit into *"Gratitude, Harmony, Intentionality, and Journaling"*? Here "harmony" refers to being congruent with what's most important to you in your life. Rather than living a haphazard life—essentially allowing the winds of change to blow you in any direction—practicing gratitude for what you already have, being intentional about your goals and how you show up in the world, and using journaling or some other form of regular reflection can help you live your best life with consistency and harmony.

Often throughout the day, I'll recall my intention/affirmation and ask myself how I'm doing with it. Occasionally I need a reminder of who and how I intended to be! More often than not, when I reflect on my day, either at the end of the day or the next morning, I recognize the ways that I did live into my intentions. By having the mindstate to be a particular way, you can live more fully the life you desire. When you invariably stray from your intention, reflection provides the opportunity to learn what and how you might approach things differently in the future.

10. *Prioritize your day.* Stephen Covey, author of *The Seven Habits of Highly Effective People,* is known for saying, "The key is not to prioritize what's on your schedule, but to schedule your priorities." In my younger years, I worked four long days and had one weekday, Monday, in which to address appointments, chores, loose ends, and more. One Monday I sat myself down in the morning after getting my young children off to elementary school and looked at my to-do list with utter despair and overwhelm. I counted no fewer than 26 items to do! It was literally a list, perhaps haphazardly and amorphously organized into a semblance of a schedule, and it was completely unrealistic. I literally set myself up for failure before ever beginning. I found myself feeling generally irritated. Starting the day with impossible expectations led to frustration. Once I could see in black-and-white writing just how ridiculously impossible it would be to accomplish the 26-item to-do list, I began to consider my priorities in a different way. What was really important to me?

In no particular order, I broke it down into a handful of areas in life: work, yoga (for me this combines physical exercise with meditation/mindfulness), finances, clutter, relationships, and myself. That pretty much covered everything that was important years ago, and I still use these categories to organize my life today, sometimes adding "movement" additionally as an opportunity to prioritize walking the dogs with my husband (that encompasses exercise and relationships!), hiking (exercise, mindfulness, and self-care), or skiing with friends (exercise and relationships).

For example, in addition to being productive in my dental office, *work* priorities might include taking an online class, writing this book, or reading a book or article related to professional growth and development. *Yoga* is generally my daily practice of mindful stretching, breathing, and strengthening, whether that is more than an hour or less than 10 minutes. *Finances* includes anything to do with making or investing money, as well as paying personal bills, sorting vendor invoices, and reviewing payroll (even though I rely on experts to manage these things). *Clutter* is my catch-all term for things that take time and need to be done, but that aren't that urgent or important to me (like doing laundry and grocery shopping). There are things that aren't glamorous or "sexy" that still need to happen.

The issue is that it's just too easy to get "busy being busy." If you're not careful, you'll occupy your waking hours with tasks that take all your time and energy and find yourself at the end of yet another day feeling exhausted and frustrated that you didn't get to do the things you would have liked to do (go for a walk, catch up with a friend, take time for a hobby, or make time for self-care). By looking at a list of these "thankless" items, it's possible to see what truly needs to get done and when, how you can be most efficient in accomplishing tasks, and what you can either get help with or just let go, realizing it's not that essential after all.

For example, if I know I have a study club or a meeting on a particular evening, I can plan to do my laundry either the night before or after the commitment, when I'll have more time available to do so, and I'll still have a clean uniform for work! If I see that I'll need to fill the car's gas tank in the next few days, pick up a few groceries, swing by the dry cleaner, and purchase dog food, I can coordinate my errands so that I do them in an order that conserves as much time and energy as possible. Maybe that dry cleaning isn't needed this week at all and can be rolled into another day or next week! Maybe instead of stopping at the pet supply store, I can order dog food online to be delivered at my convenience. When I found myself scrubbing the bathroom at 10 o'clock at night, I conceded that it might make more sense for my well-being to pay for someone to help with basic house cleaning every other week, freeing me up to relax before bed or just get to sleep on time.

But what if you're barely making ends meet and can't afford to hire help? Is there someone else you can ask to pitch in with the responsibilities? If you are a single parent of small children and taking care of the house is up to you, maybe you plan to just clean the toilet one day and the bathtub a different day so it's not so overwhelming. By scheduling your priorities, you give yourself permission to *not* have to do everything at the same time or on the same day. When you plan to do laundry on Wednesday and you find yourself looking at the pile of dirty clothes on Tuesday, thinking that you *could* keep going just a bit more, being intentional with your time allows you the freedom to grant yourself permission to relax and have some time for your own well-being by *not* doing the laundry a day early.

Are you starting to get the picture? By dumping out all the to-dos for the week, you can see what really needs to get done and when/how is the best time/way.

Relationships shouldn't be on your to-do list—or should they? For me, I consider which relationships might need me the most and what they might need more of from me, and make these people a planned part of my life. What does that look like? Perhaps your neighbor's parent is going through chemotherapy, so you just remind yourself to check in to see how everyone is doing. Or you know that your coworker's child had a birthday party and you remind yourself to ask about it. Maybe you haven't heard from a family member who lives far away in awhile. You could remind yourself (in your daily calendar or schedule) to reach out with a text or call, letting them know that you're thinking of them.

Then there are the more obvious relationships, the people with whom you are closest—your family, friends, and significant others. It goes without saying that life can get busy, and the danger is in neglecting your relationships. Just like physical fitness cannot be stored without continuous effort, like plants need to be watered and weeded in order to thrive, and like you need to practice a musical instrument regularly in order to play at your best, relationships also require consistent attention and nurturing in order to thrive. Making a conscious effort to plan lunch or a walk to catch up with your friends, spending time playing with your children or pets, and making regular dates with your significant other are essential!

Does that mean that your whole life needs to be planned? Of course not—being spontaneous is beautiful! It's just that spontaneity by its very nature is unpredictable. You can't rely solely on moment-to-moment inspiration to maintain your critical relationships. Intentionally planning time with certain people shows that your relationships are important to you. And looking forward to a family outing on the weekend, dinner with a friend, or a weekend away with your significant other brings joy and connection to everyone!

Finally, *myself* is the most challenging item on my priority list. It's simply too easy to get busy doing everything else except make time for me, and that's why I do it. Taking care of myself includes things like making sure I keep up with my well visits and screening appointments (mammograms, colonoscopy, dermatology, ophthalmology, bloodwork, etc.), as well as making time for having my hair done and an occasional pedicure. *Myself* includes making time for healthy meals (literally some days I realize I'm running from one appointment to another without allotting time to eat lunch!), for leisure/hobbies (I like doing jigsaw puzzles just for the fun of it), and for winding down at the end of the day so I can enjoy a good sleep.

As you can see, the possibilities are endless! Being intentional and scheduling your priorities does not mean being rigidly planned 24/7. On the contrary, being intentional gives you the freedom to be flexible! Knowing what's truly important versus what can wait for another day allows you to make changes in your plan as the day unfolds; it allows you to know when you might need to ramp things up a bit, and when you can relax and give yourself a break because enough is enough, and you are enough. The take-home message is to identify what's most important to you and then prioritize those areas of your life intentionally.

CONCLUSION: PUTTING IT ALL TOGETHER

Congratulations! You've already accomplished a great deal of learning and self-inquiry. And what's next? Go back through the chapters, especially "Points to Ponder," and reflect on what has changed for you. What new understanding have you acquired? What new tools are in your self-care toolbelt? What new awareness do you bring to everyday life? And what commitments have you made to *yourself* to practice self-awareness, self-care, and self-compassion? This work is transformational, whether through a giant "aha" moment or more gradually and incrementally. In a nutshell:

- Live in gratitude and harmony.
- Cultivate self-awareness, practice self-care and compassion.
- Be mindful and intentional.
- Stretch yourself, physically and mentally.
- Re-read this book, because as you grow, new insights will emerge.

And please reach out to me to let me know how you're doing and what you're working on. Additionally, if you'd like me to speak to your organization or you'd like to join in one of the workshops I offer throughout the year, contact me on my website www.drrobertagarceau.com.

Truly wishing you *Bliss, Not Burnout*.

Namaste

REVIEW INQUIRY

Hey, it's Roberta here. I hope you've enjoyed the book, finding it both useful and fun!

I have a small favor to ask. Would you consider giving *Bliss, Not Burnout* a rating wherever you purchased it? Online bookstores are more likely to promote a book when they feel good about its content, and reader reviews are a great barometer for a book's quality.

So please go to the website of wherever you bought the book, search for my name and the book title, and leave a review. If able, perhaps consider adding a picture of you holding the book. That increases the likelihood your review will be accepted!

With much gratitude in advance,

Roberta Garceau

WILL YOU SHARE THE LOVE?

Get this book for a friend, associate, or family member!

If you've found *Bliss, Not Burnout* to be valuable, would you consider gifting a copy to your personal health care providers or to a special health care provider in your family, friend group, or community? You'll be helping the world to be a better place!

WOULD YOU LIKE ROBERTA GARCEAU TO SPEAK TO YOUR ORGANIZATION?

Book Roberta Now!

Roberta Garceau accepts a limited number of speaking/teaching/training engagements each year. To learn how you can bring her message to your organization, email roberta@drrobertagarceau.com or visit www.drrobertagarceau.com.

ABOUT THE AUTHOR

Dr. Roberta Garceau is a practicing dentist, certified yoga and āyurveda instructor, professional speaker, and a diplomate of the American Board of Dental Sleep Medicine. She blends these passions into Elemental-Wellness, her unique brand of integrative medicine, to help others improve their health, function, self-esteem, and overall well-being.

As a practicing dentist for over 25 years, Dr. Garceau has embraced modern science and medicine as we know it today, and she continues to study the latest advancements in the field in order to bring her best to her patients and her work team. From the beginning, she appreciated the connection between oral and systemic health, as well as mental and emotional health. Dr. Garceau has led workshops on Elemental-Wellness for rising health care providers—both medical and dental students at the University of Connecticut. She has also presented to dentists at various study clubs, teams at the California Dental Association, physician assistants at the Connecticut Academy of PAs, and other health care providers through Professional Learning Services.

Whether sharing her weekly MyYogaJoy videos, leading her workshops, or speaking and presenting to other groups, Roberta is passionate about fostering self-awareness and lifting others so they may empower themselves to live with greater wellness.

She and her husband, Jerry, reside in Connecticut and enjoy spending time both outdoors in nature and with their adult children, Jacenda and Liam (as well as their labradoodles!).

For upcoming presentations and workshops, you can contact her through her website www.drrobertagarceau.com.

www.ingramcontent.com/pod-product-compliance
Lightning Source LLC
Chambersburg PA
CBHW080755120626
46557CB00006B/1278